WE WERE HOOKED

Harold Flender talked with more than three hundred young people in twenty-five drug-treatment centers from California to Connecticut. This book consists of tape-recorded interviews with thirteen of them, aged 13 to 27, who had been free of drugs for periods ranging from four months to five years.

These ex-addicts explain how and why they got into drugs. They describe the world of the addict, a world where getting drugs is all that matters—sometimes through forged prescriptions, shoplifting, hustling, drug pushing or armed robbery. And they tell of the growing problems that finally led to the decision to "kick."

The thirteen, who were chosen to illustrate different ways of getting off drugs, are not always in agreement about what works.

They don't know what will help anyone else. They only know what helped them.

WE WERE

HOOKED

Thirteen young ex-addicts tell about their experiences
with heroin, LSD, speed, and other drugs
and how they kicked the habit.
Interviews and foreword by Harold Flender

Random House/New York

Copyright © 1972 by Harold Flender. All rights re-
served under International and Pan-American Copy-
right Conventions. Published in the United States by
Random House, Inc., New York, and simultaneously
in Canada by Random House of Canada Limited,
Toronto.
Library of Congress Cataloging in Publication Data
Main entry under title: We were hooked.
1. Drugs and youth—United States. 2. Drug abuse—
Treatment—United States. I. Flender, Harold.
HV5825.W383   362.2′93′0926   72–1589
ISBN 0–394–82376–1 ISBN 0–394–92376–6(lib. bdg.)
Manufactured in the United States of America

For Nicole and Rodman

Contents

being alone, even in a locked cell, had a great deal to do with it.

MITCHELL 77

For about six years I'd been a heavy drug user. I got out of drugs completely on my own. However, once I was off drugs, I did get into a wonderful program to help me stay off drugs.

MARIO 89

I got started on drugs when I was in Vietnam. With just straight psychiatric care, I'd get more hooked than ever. But with methadone and group therapy, I'd say the results have been excellent.

GLORIA 95

I couldn't see how I could live without the drugs. I was hunting for peace. I found it, the happiness, the joy, the completeness. The Lord has come into my life.

BILL 109

Cyclazocine is not a magic pill. You must have therapy to go along with it. Otherwise there won't be sufficient motivation to get off drugs and stay off.

DANIEL 117

I had set very high goals for myself. I was looking for some kind of perfection, some kind of answer. I had no real idea who I was. I thought maybe I'd get some insight through drugs.

SUSAN 131

I realized that I never got anything out of taking the tranquilizers, the amphetamines, the barbiturates. I got off drugs because I was able to suddenly grow up a bit and face reality. I also got tired of serving time in prison.

Foreword

To obtain material for this book, I visited twenty-five drug-treatment centers in California, New Mexico, Colorado, Texas, Illinois, New York, Connecticut, and Washington, D.C. At the treatment centers I talked with more than three hundred young people.

This book consists of tape-recorded interviews with thirteen of them who had been free of drugs for periods ranging from four months to five years. The thirteen were chosen to illustrate different ways of getting off drugs. The words in the interviews are those of the young people themselves. Names have been changed, and sometimes biographical details, to keep individuals from being recognized.

These ex-addicts are not always in agreement about what works. Some of them believe in strict rules for a treatment center, while others favor a relaxed atmosphere. Some, but not all, feel that encounter groups are effective. There is strong disagreement about methadone.

Some of them have been helped by psychiatrists; others are scornful of psychiatry. One ex-addict believes the only answer is Jesus, and another believes just as strongly in Yoga.

These young people don't know what will help anyone else. They only know what helped them. "There is no one answer and certainly no magic solution," says Susan.

"I can't speak for some other person," says George, "because I don't have the feelings and emotions of another person." Ex-addicts sometimes explain the varieties of effective treatment with the expression "Different strokes for different folks."

Perhaps they come closest to agreement when they mention the need to take responsibility for one's own life. "To get off drugs," says Timmy, "you have to make up your mind that it's really what you want to do. Nobody can make you give up drugs except yourself."

It is easy to get hooked. It is much more difficult to get unhooked. Few actually make it. However, as these interviews show, it is not impossible. Various kinds of help are available. "Once you really are ready to be helped," says Susan, "then you can be."

WE WERE HOOKED

DINA

Basically I was a speed freak. Being able to talk about our problems has helped me change. If you have people, you don't need drugs.

Dina, who started on drugs at the age of fifteen, comes from an industrial city in Connecticut. Her interview takes place at Project Renaissance in West-port, a commuter town near New York City. Located in a former store, Project Renaissance is available to anyone who wants to join.

A slender brunette with long hair and blue eyes, Dina is wearing a sweater, blue jeans and sandals. She has a relaxed, matter-of-fact way of telling her story.

I started on drugs two years ago, because I wanted to get in with the crowd of people I felt were cool.

I started in tenth grade, and my first experience with drugs was in smoking grass. After a few months I was smoking it every day. I was enjoying the high I got, but pretty soon I also began getting paranoid. We'd be sitting in someone's apartment smoking grass, and suddenly this big fear would come over me that someone might break in and something bad would happen.

My parents didn't know that I was into drugs, or didn't want to know. They suspected what was going on but were too afraid to confront me with it. Many times I'd stay out all night and wouldn't come home, but it was like they were scared to talk to me about it. A couple of times my father even asked me if I was using drugs. But when I told him no, he seemed satisfied.

They weren't too hip to what was going on, because they are both from Germany. My father is a truck driver and my mother a teller in a bank.

I have an older sister, a real goody-goody girl who went to college and never had anything to do with drugs.

My parents were always saying things like, "Why can't you be like your sister?" This would piss me off because I didn't care for my sister and her way of life. She's never had a life of her own. With her it was always, "Yes, ma . . . no, ma . . . whatever you say, ma." I had no respect for her because she let my mother run her life.

I'm different. I like making up my own mind, making my own decisions. I want to experience my own things. My mother would like me to go to school, then work at a job for a while, and finally, when I'm twenty-five years old, find a nice Jewish boy and get married. I can't see it that way. I figure that if I'm going to fall in love, it's going to be with whomever I happen to fall in love, not necessarily a nice Jewish boy. But my mother can't see this at all, just as she can't see a lot of my other ideas. I really think this was one reason I took to drugs.

Trying to get in with a crowd in order to have friends was another reason for drugs, probably the most important reason. I began to go steady with this boy I met in high school. He was into shooting speed. At first I was afraid to fool around with it, even by popping pills. But then when I got in with my boyfriend's crowd of people, I felt I had to do what they were doing, so I began taking other drugs. I began tripping with acid. It was at this time that my grades in school started going down. Somehow I managed to pass my tenth grade, but my marks were really way down.

Smoking grass makes you very hungry, and I gained a lot of weight from overeating. I knew that amphetamines were used to make you lose weight, so I began taking them. It wasn't long before I realized that I really dug amphetamines. At first, two would get me off for the whole day. But the trouble with amphetamines is that you gradually build up a resistance to them, and it wasn't long before I was taking twenty to thirty amphetamines a day.

One of the things I liked about grass and amphetamines was that they made sex easier. I was always afraid of sex until I started smoking grass. That loosened me up and made it easier for me to have sex with my boyfriend. And if my boyfriend wasn't around, I'd go out with some other guy and have sex.

I didn't have to buy too often. Most of the time my friends would give me drugs, or I'd steal them from other users, or I'd have sex with guys in exchange for drugs. I also did some dealing in acid so I could get money for speed. In addition to popping amphetamine pills like Dexedrine, I also started in with Methedrine, first snorting it and then shooting it.

Basically I was a speed freak, but once in a while I still tripped on acid. One day I was crashing or coming down from speed when I decided to trip with some acid. Unfortunately, I was with the wrong guy at the time. You have to be with the right person when you drop acid or it can be a very bad trip. This time I was with a guy who messed with my head and he really flipped me out.

He had taken me to his house when we took the acid and suddenly in the middle of the trip he wanted to ball me. When I refused, he started knocking me around, really beating me up. His treatment of me really flipped me out. I didn't know what I was doing. A really bad trip. I didn't know whether I was coming or going.

When he saw the way I was acting, he got scared, because he thought he had really hurt me. He split, leaving me all alone in his house. His mother came home. When she saw me in the house, not knowing who I was, she called the police. They took me to the hospital. It took me about thirty to forty hours to come down from that trip. It was a really bad trip with all kinds of hallucinations.

Finally, when I came out of it, I saw that my mother and father were at my bedside in the hospital. In the back of their minds they had known for a while that I had been using drugs. But this was their first real proof of it, and I could see that it was a real slap in the face to them. I mean, the police had picked both of them up at work to bring them to the hospital.

They started carrying on, asking me why I had taken drugs. But I only told them that I promised that I would never take drugs again. They believed me, only because they wanted to believe me. I couldn't understand their believing me so easily, because I felt it was very obvious that I was lying. I had no intention of stopping drugs. I figured maybe I would never trip any more, but I would still take speed. Maybe I might also take mescaline once in a while even if I cut out acid.

They kept me in the hospital a week, and then I went home. As soon as I got home I started right in with drugs again. My boyfriend came over with a lot of barbiturates and we both got caught by my father. When he saw that we were both under the influence of drugs, he got really mad and beat me up. He then had me committed to a state mental hospital.

It was at the mental hospital that I started using heroin. All sorts of drugs were easy to get there. But mainly I was still into speed. When they saw what was happening, they switched me over to a drug program they had there. There it was more difficult to get drugs. What was even worse was that I was in with a lot of real dope fiends, people who had been shooting dope for a long time.

Finally, a social worker took pity on me and arranged for me to get into Project Renaissance here at Westport.

What I liked about Project Renaissance was that I wasn't locked up or confined. I could live out and just come here three nights a week. I thought that this would be a great opportunity for me to get back on drugs easily. And it would also be good to be able to be back with my old man again.

I went back to living with my parents. Every Monday, Wednesday, and Friday I'd come to Project Renaissance from 6:30 to 11 P.M.

The first thing I'd have to do when I got here was

to help clean the place. Then we'd have seminars and a house meeting. We'd go over the routine here, what we were expected to do, the purpose of it, how it was supposed to help us. We would sometimes discuss world affairs and current events that affected our lives, such as the war in Vietnam. The "pull-ups" would consist of making you aware of what you were doing wrong, especially if your attitude was wrong.

After the house meeting, we'd have the encounter groups, and they are really the biggest and most important part of the therapy here. At the groups, anything goes except physical violence or the threat of physical violence. But you can say anything to anyone in the group, yell at anyone you want, really get close to your feelings.

On the outside, if somebody hurts you, you might want to run away from the unpleasantness of the situation by taking drugs. It's an escape from reality. But here in the groups, they try to get you to face reality by facing the fact that somebody has hurt your feelings and letting them know in no uncertain terms that they've done it.

When I first started coming here it wasn't easy. The change in me didn't happen right away like magic. For one thing, I still had my old man and he was still on drugs. He was still getting high and a few times after I started in here I even got high with him.

I copped to the group here what I was doing. They pointed out to me in plain language that if I really wanted to kick drugs the first thing I'd have to do was to cut loose from my old man. It wasn't easy to do. I messed up a few times and had to wear a dunce cap.

I wouldn't face the fact that I was a messed-up person. I always thought I was together. I finally realized it wasn't true. After about a month, I realized that I couldn't keep sitting on the fence. Either I was going to go back to being a speed freak or I was going to cut my old man loose. I decided finally to clean up my own mess, and I cut him loose. When I made that decision, I realized that that was the first time in my life that I had started caring about myself.

I said to myself, "Dig it! Why are you here? You shouldn't even be here. If you didn't do all of these messed-up things in the first place, you would never have gotten here." And then I started thinking that as long as I was here, I might as well try to bring myself back to being a human being again.

I felt pretty bad about myself. But I also realized that I was a person and had to start feeling like a person. I had to get myself together. I had to look at some of the problems I had inside of me and take care of them. At that point, I knew that getting high was not good for me and something I no longer wanted to do any more. Getting high was not going to solve any problems for me.

In group, I saw that to help me solve my problems I needed people rather than drugs, the people who were here. If you have people, you don't need drugs.

In addition to coming here regularly three times a week you can come here anytime you want to, just to rap to people about your problems. I would say that after group, that's about the most important part of the program here at Project Renaissance. If you have problems with your parents or a boyfriend or you mess up in any area, you can always come here any time you want to, day or night, and find someone to rap with instead of taking drugs.

Another part of the therapy here is doing what we call "Image Blowers." This is a fun thing, because you can't be serious all the time. My image was always that of someone very conservative, very serious. But in Image Blowers, say you have to imitate an ostrich laying an egg. That not only is funny and makes everybody laugh, but it's good for you because it loosens you up and makes you less uptight and blows your image.

In the few months that I was at the mental hospital, I saw a psychiatrist only twice. The first time was for about a minute, when I was admitted. The second time was for about four minutes. That was when they found out I was taking drugs at the hospital and they transferred me to the drug program. Otherwise, all you saw at the mental hospital were nurses and attendants, mainly attendants.

The people who really run the place here at Project Renaissance House are all ex-addicts. In addition, Project Renaissance has an advisory board, which has some psychiatrists on it. These psychiatrists are available for those kids here who may have special problems and feel they need that kind of help.

I've been coming to Project Renaissance for a year now, and I have been off drugs all this time. I've also been able to go back to high school. And, much to everybody's surprise, my marks have been higher than ever. I'll be graduating this year. I guess I've proved to people that I'm not all that stupid.

I don't know yet what I'll be doing after high school. Maybe in a few years I'll go to college. Right now I'm not ready for it. After the summer I'll probably go to work in a new live-in facility that Project Renaissance is starting upstate. In helping others who are in trouble with drugs, I believe I'll be helping myself a great deal. I still need a lot of strength. I don't think I'm strong enough to be sure I'll be able to stay away from drugs for the rest of my life, not to try to get high again on speed.

If I did go to college, I would want to major in

psychology. Knowing psychology would help me in helping other people. The only purpose in life now for me is to help myself and to help other people.

One of the reasons I don't feel like going into college right after I graduate from high school is that I'm down on schools in general because I think they are pretty cruddy places for communicating. For instance, two weeks ago a friend of mine died from O.D.ing. When I found out about it, I was naturally all shook up.

I heard about it while I was in school. There was nobody there, I really mean nobody, that I could speak to about it who would understand what I was going through and would try to help me. I even tried going to the guidance counselor at the school. I started crying and carrying on before her, but she really didn't know where I was at and what it was all about.

Schools should be places where people can learn to communicate with each other. But, instead, schools are actually more like jails. Nobody talks freely in schools. When they do talk, they talk about their boyfriends or their girlfriends or drugs. They really never talk about the most important thing of all—themselves—just superficial things.

When I talk to my friends here at Project Renaissance, I can talk about my insecurities, my inadequacies, all the things that make me feel that I'm not a good person, all the things that I don't like about myself. It's only by talking about these things to others and getting them out into the open that you can do something about them.

Here we really know how to communicate and help each other with our problems. One problem I had a lot of help with here was my bitchiness. Before I came here, I was very selfish. I didn't care about anybody. I used to feel very bad about being such a bitch. But it wasn't until I came here and started to face up to it in the group encounters that I was able to do anything about it. Being able to talk freely about our problems the way we can here has helped me change. Once in a while I do fall back and act mean like a bitch, but I'm not nearly as bad as I used to be.

It's not an easy thing to do, to talk honestly to other people about your feelings. I could never do it on the outside. However, when you see the others doing it here, it makes it easier for you to do it. The more you work at it, the easier it becomes to do.

And you don't take all your problems at once. You take them one at a time. After you solve one, you go on to the next one. My bitchiness was one problem, my relations with my parents another one.

Right now I'm back living with my folks. We still can't communicate with one another, and I know we never will, but I also know that I love them and they love me. At the same time, I realize that while we love each other we just cannot live together. It's a fact of life I just have to face. That's one of the reasons I'm looking forward to the possibility of working in the new live-in facility of Project Renaissance upstate. It'll mean being able to move out of my parents' house.

Some of the kids here have better luck with their parents. Their parents are more understanding. There are regular meetings between staff and parents, which help the parents very much. Unfortunately, they didn't seem to help my parents. But that's the way it is.

There are about seventy of us connected with Project Renaissance, and I can honestly say that I think the thing is really working for practically all of us. A lot of us here really never had friends. We are basically lonely people. Here we were able to form close friendships for the first time in our lives.

Some of the kids who come to this place have never taken drugs but are afraid they might. For them, this place is like preventive medicine. Maybe if there had been a place like this for me two years ago, I never would have started in with drugs.

In addition to seeing each other here, we also go out together. We go to movies, go bowling together, and so forth. We become dependent on each other, but it's only for a while, until we are ready to go out into the community again.

We try to get people to grow emotionally—to be able to deal with the basic feelings of love, fear, hostility, and happiness. People here learn how to care, how to be sensitive, how to be men and women instead of children.

Before settling down, before even going to college, I would like to travel. One of the places I'd like to visit is Israel. I think I'd like to try living on a kibbutz, because on a kibbutz you're all working for each other. I think I would find that kind of environment very good.

The environment most of us are in here in the United States is too much of a rat race. Everybody is competing with everybody else instead of cooperating and helping. It's this rat race that causes a lot of kids to drop out of society and turn to drugs. People here strive only for material things and status. I don't think it will be that way on a kibbutz in Israel.

And, who knows, maybe on a kibbutz I'll be able to meet a nice Jewish boy and get married and settle down.

JOHN

A lot of people think that all junkies are thieves and murderers. But they're not. Many of them just want a chance to start all over again.

John is thirteen and small for his age. His parents are from Puerto Rico. His father is a New York City fireman.

John is a member of the Rutgers Community Center's drug-prevention program on New York's Lower East Side. He wears chinos, a Hawaiian sport shirt, a black sweater and white sneakers. His hair, at his father's insistence, is unfashionably short.

I started messing around with drugs when I was ten. First I used smoke. You know, marijuana. We call it smoke. I got it from my friends in public school. They used to give it to me, to turn me on, for free. I never had to pay for it.

I thought it was a big thing, because all my friends were doing it. We used to get high on smoke mainly at this one friend's house, when his mother wasn't there. Like, his father died. So his mother goes out and works and nobody's home, so we smoke it there.

Then my friend, he gave me some pills. I don't know what they were. But I didn't like them. They were supposed to get you high, but all they did for me was give me the cold sweats and make me throw up. So I stopped taking them and went back to smoke until I got into snort. That's heroin. It's called snort when you snort it into your nostrils. It's called smack, or whatever you want to call it, when you shoot it.

I used heroin to get away from my problems and everything, problems at home, my mother and father. Like, my sisters used to get a lot of things, right? I have five sisters. But I'm the only boy. My mother liked my sisters. They used to take everything out on me. They would yell at me and everything.

I just got sick and tired of it. I would stay out of the house as much as possible. But every time I would come home late, my father would hit me. I told him I wasn't a kid no more. But he kept hitting me. Every time I got into a fight with my sisters, my mother and father would never do anything to them, but they would hit me. So I would go downstairs and get high on my snort and forget about all my problems.

I was on snort for about a year, but I got high one night, right? And I went to this place where we used to hang out on Grand Street. I was eating a hamburger and then I looked at it, and the ketchup looked like blood. I threw up right there, and the owner thought it was the hamburger that had made me sick, so he gave me my money back. I left the store. Then I went and lay down on a park bench, threw up the rest of my guts, and then I went and drank some milk, because I knew that milk would make me feel better. Then I went home and went to sleep.

It was around this time that all sorts of things began happening that made me afraid of what I was doing. Like, at school they started showing these movies on what happens to you when you take drugs. They were very scary. Then they had speakers come over, ex-addicts, right? They told how they had been in jail and all the terrible things that happened to them.

And then I saw one of my best friends O.D. He was trying to get the vein in his arm with an eyedropper. He kept missing. Making all those holes in his arm and no vein. Then he finally hit and the blood went into the spike and up the eyedropper. Next thing I knew he was out cold right on the staircase where he had been shooting up.

They dragged him out. They tried to give him milk, but he couldn't swallow it. They slapped him and everything, but they couldn't wake him up. They called an ambulance, and when it came they tried giving him five of those little things with ammonia in them to wake him up, and he still didn't wake up. Then they put him in the ambulance and took him up to the hospital. I heard he was unconscious for two days, and then he died.

When I heard he was dead, I said, "No, this is it. I ain't doing it no more." All these things, when I thought the ketchup on the hamburger was blood and I got sick, when I saw the movies and heard the ex-addicts at school, when I saw with my own eyes what happened to my friend—all these things made me scared and want to stop.

Then I heard about the drug-prevention program at the Rutgers Community Center on Madison Street. Some of my friends were going there and said it was real good in keeping them out of trouble and off drugs. So I went there with them. They got a program that keeps you off the street, like, so you don't get a bag. You get a ball to play with instead of a bag. We had gym, we had art, we had black history, Puerto Rican history, we had things like that. It was an after-school program, except for the summer, when we went all day. It kept me off the street, it kept me from getting high, so I kept going. And during the summer another thing we had was bus trips out of the city.

In addition to all of the activities, like, they talked to you and everything. They helped you out with your family problems and everything. They speak to your family, too. So I stayed. It was nice.

What do I think really got me off drugs? Like I said, it was mainly being scared, seeing what happened to my friend who died, the movies and the guys talking at the school. Sure, the Rutgers Community Center helped a lot by keeping me off the streets. It's a wonderful program. It's really drug prevention.

A lot of people want to close down these places. Right away a lot of people think that all junkies are thieves and murderers. But they're not. Many of them just want a chance to start all over again. If they close down these places, they won't be able to start all over again, like me. I guess they'll just end up in jail.

I've been off drugs, let's see, Christmas should be about a year.

ROSITA

Wanting to quit and being able to kick are two different things. I guess you could say that falling in love and wanting to get married is what made me stop.

Rosita is a Chicano from Denver, Colorado. She now lives in Santa Fe, New Mexico, where she attends a treatment center known as "El Vicio"—Spanish for "The Vice." Rosita's vice was heroin.

Rosita has long dark hair and brown eyes. She smiles easily both at the interviewer and at her boyfriend, who holds her hand throughout the interview.

I started with drugs when I was thirteen. My two older brothers were heroin addicts.

All my life we lived in the Chicano section of Denver, where there was always plenty of heroin around. There were four or five heroin pushers on my block alone. It seemed like everybody was on it.

I started with pills. Mostly Seconals, reds. I also smoked a lot of grass, starting at about thirteen.

When I was a little kid I used to see my brothers fixing, and I wondered about it. They started shooting it when they were about fourteen or fifteen. They never told me what they were really doing. When I'd catch them at it, they'd say that they were taking shots for vitamins or hay fever or something like that. That's what they used to say, or they'd chase me out of the room.

At first, my parents didn't know about my brothers. They knew what was going on in the neighborhood, but they didn't know that my brothers were using dope at that time. Later they found out. They weren't shocked, because they knew how that neighborhood was. It's one of the worst ones in Denver. They didn't throw my brothers out of the house or anything. They tried to tell them not to use dope, but they never threw them out of the house.

We were a welfare family. My father used to work as a civilian employee on an Army base near Denver. Then he got sick. A couple of weeks before he was supposed to retire they fired him, and he didn't get his pension. He had no choice but to go on welfare. We are Chicanos, and almost all the Chicanos in our neighborhood were on welfare—on welfare and on drugs.

I actually didn't get involved with hard drugs in Denver, but in Los Angeles. I knew all about them in Denver, but I didn't start using them until I finished high school and moved with a girlfriend to Los Angeles. I was seventeen. We wanted to get some grass, but we couldn't find a connection right away. The people who lived next door to us in L.A. used heroin and they were always at our house, so we started using it, too.

Originally my girlfriend and I had gone to California to look for work, but we couldn't find a job anywhere. I could type with one finger, but everyplace wanted shorthand and this and that. We tried the telephone company, too. But nobody would hire us.

We finally stopped looking and ended up partying all the time. Partying and taking dope. We got so disgusted because nobody would hire us that we started selling dope ourselves to make a living. Luckily, we never had to hustle, because we could always sell enough dope to support our habits. We did do a lot of shoplifting, though.

What got me started on heroin was being so disgusted with life. I had left this really bad neighborhood in Denver, where nobody would give you a chance, and come all the way to California. And nobody would give me a chance there either. I just couldn't get a job. They always said they wanted somebody with some experience. Well, how could I get some experience if nobody would hire me for my first job?

So I said, "I don't care, I'm just going to forget about everybody else." And as long as I was on heroin I forgot about everybody else. It really worked, you know?

Heroin was really easy to get in L.A. It was always available. It took me about a year to get really hooked, because at first I'd use it only off and on. By the time I was eighteen, I was really hooked.

Oh, another thing I liked about heroin was that it

made me forget about sex. At the time I was really down on guys, because I'd gotten screwed around a lot and burned. As long as I was stoned, I didn't care about guys, not at all.

One day, about a year ago, I decided to go down to Mexico, because I heard the heroin was pure down there and easy to get. So I went to this place on the Pacific coast near Acapulco where I lived for eight months.

I found what I'd heard about the heroin in Mexico was no exaggeration. Down there the stuff is really pure. I was stoned all the time. By the time I got back to L.A., I had a really bad habit. It was terrible, because in Mexico I had gotten used to this pure stuff. And in L.A. I was only able to get stuff that was cut a lot. Still, I couldn't get off, so I had to spend more and more money back in L.A.

I also began to have this terrible fear of running out and not being able to get more. When you're an addict, you just have to get it, you know? So I got really heavy into shoplifting and even begging. I mean, God, I was spending over a thousand dollars a month just on my habit. And what did I have to show for it?

I really began to get tired of L.A. I mean, it was just so awful and all the heroin I needed was getting harder to get and everything was going wrong there. So I came back to Denver, still very much hooked.

My parents were really broken up when they saw I had returned from L.A. a heroin addict. I've always had good relations with my parents, mainly I guess because I'm the only girl. They've always loved me and been kind to me, and I've always loved them.

It used to hurt me real bad when I took drugs because I knew it was hurting them. But it had nothing to do with them that I was taking drugs. I just couldn't help it. I tried to explain to them not to feel hurt for me. They thought that by telling me, "We love you," and, "Please get off of it," that I could do it. But I couldn't, you know?

It was shortly after I came back to Denver that I met this fellow at a party. We started going out and I fell in love with him. He was a manager of a bowling alley, and he knew I was an addict. He took real good care of me. We decided that we wanted to get married, but first he wanted me to get off heroin. I figured that he's done so much for me that I'm going to quit for him.

He told me about the methadone program in Denver. I knew something about it, because one of my brothers had gotten off drugs through that program. However, my boyfriend and I had by that time decided to move from Denver to Santa Fe. We learned that there was a similar program here in Santa Fe. I figured I would try it. If I didn't like it, I could always quit. So I started here in El Vicio, and I really like it. It's really helped me out. I've been straight now for four months, ever since I started.

I guess you could say that falling in love and wanting to get married was what made me stop. But I'm really not sure, because when you're an addict that stuff makes you really selfish. After you get hooked, you can only be in love with that needle. You can't really be in love with or even care for anybody else. The only thing you care about is that you get that fix and that's it.

Maybe what really made me want to stop was all the money that my habit was using up for stuff that was cut so much it wasn't any good.

Another important reason is that the girls I knew who were on the stuff looked real old compared to the age they really were. I was thinking that pretty soon if I didn't get off it I'd be looking like I was forty years old. I didn't want my looks to get all messed up, and I knew that heroin really does mess up the way you look.

All these things, I guess—worrying about the money, the lack of good stuff available, worrying about getting messed up, and wanting very much to do something for my boyfriend because I was in love with him and he had done so much for me—all of these things made me want to quit.

But wanting to quit and being able to kick are two different things, and it is the methadone program that has made it possible for me to quit. I come in every morning for my methadone and orange juice. It really keeps you from wanting to fix. And anything that can do that, I've got to say, "Man, that's something else!" Because I've never known anything else that works. And it works not only for me but for a lot of my friends who are also on the program.

Remember I told you that a lot of other Chicanos from the slums were on heroin? Well, a lot of them are now off heroin, thanks to methadone. It's really the only thing that works, I think, because it works on the body, and being an addict is a physical thing.

When you're sick, you're sick, and that's all there is to it. Methadone keeps you from getting sick. It's not in your mind. Once you're hooked, it's in your body.

Eventually, I hope to get off methadone. They say you can, you know.

My boyfriend and I are planning to get married soon.

JACK

While you're a speed freak, you take anything you can get your hands on. I knew I really wanted to get off drugs. But it wasn't until I was into Yoga that I was able to get off all drugs.

Jack studies Yoga at Horizon Center, a program in New York's Greenwich Village, funded by the city and federal governments.

In the studio where he is interviewed, there is on the wall a large poster showing a lotus flower. Around the flower are the words "Truth, Knowledge, Bliss."

Jack is tall, thin, smiles a lot. He is calm and seems very much in control. He wears blue jeans, a white T-shirt and love beads.

I'm eighteen years old. The first drug I got into was grass, when I was fifteen years old and going to high school. I started at first to be in with the other students. Then I began buying it and smoking it alone.

My background is solid middle class. My father is a lawyer and my mother is a secretary at a foundation. I have two younger sisters.

There was nothing I was really missing at home. We lived in a very nice two-family house. I had a good relationship with my folks. We were a close family. I was a very good student. School did bother me, though. It was one of my problems. I felt I always had to have the highest marks at school. This pressure did not come from my folks. It was inside me.

Somehow I became interested in living a different kind of life, and got very curious about marijuana. But I really can't say that I started changing my life style and getting into marijuana because there were problems that I wanted to get away from, like the pressure of always maintaining high grades. I really feel, now that I think about it, that it was more wanting to find something that I felt was missing, something I needed in life. I thought grass would help me to fit into a different life style, that it would give me a different image of myself.

I wanted to feel that I was really a part of the underground. I felt I couldn't identify with the Establishment. There were a lot of Establishment things that people in my own peer group were into that I didn't like—for example, the whole business of the way people went out on dates and decided to go steady. Then there were the kids whom I considered super-robots in terms of school. All they did was work very hard to get good grades at school. I myself was a super-robot, but I didn't want to be one.

I did have an interest in the music thing that was

around at the time, particularly Bob Dylan. I really got into Bob Dylan's alienation thing.

Once I was heavily into grass I was able to change my whole attitude towards school. I didn't really care about working hard to get marks. In my junior year I almost flunked out. I got into a real negative head about school, about myself, about a lot of things. I wasn't digging myself at all.

A few of my friends started using LSD. At first I didn't want to get into LSD. I thought it would be too heavy. But eventually I tried it, and when I found out that I didn't freak out on it I began taking LSD pretty regularly. At first I would trip only weekends, then I began tripping during the week. I guess over a period of two or three months I tripped about fifty-five or sixty times, which isn't a whole lot compared to the way some people trip.

Acid, like pot, was very easy to get at school. There was a regular drug culture at that high school, which I understand has become a lot bigger than it was when I started about three years ago. We didn't even have to buy drugs. We were a group of friends who supplied each other. For a while acid seemed to supply the missing thing that I was looking for, certainly more so than grass. While I hadn't had any bad trips on LSD, there were a couple of times when coming down made me feel insecure, and that I might be losing my mind.

When I went from LSD to speed, I didn't feel, at first, at all scared. When you're on speed you feel so high, you feel that you're never going to come down. You also feel when you take speed that nothing can go wrong. At first I started in by taking uppers— pills, Benzedrine, Dexedrine, Dexamyl, Methedrine. I suppose I hit about every combination of uppers possible.

One thing about speed, though, is that you develop a tolerance to it rather quickly. After a while, in order to have that nice feeling all the time, you have to go into something heavier than pills. That's when I became a speed freak, and began buying it by the spoonful. It cost about twenty-five dollars for a spoonful in powder form. I began by snorting and ended up by shooting. All told, I was a speed freak for about six months.

I was acting crazy. I wasn't sleeping. I wasn't eating. I had dropped out of school.

When you're on speed you really are a freak and a lunatic. Speed is too much for your body and mind to handle. On speed you are more mentally active than you've been in your whole life. But your mind really can't take it. Your body can't take it either, because, in addition to not eating properly and not getting enough sleep, you're putting all of this poison into you. That's why among drug abusers there are more deaths among speed freaks than heroin addicts.

In addition to the serious damage speed does to the nervous system and to the rest of the body—you can actually hear your heart going a mile a minute—there's the psychological effect of the crash. When you're on speed you feel that you are never going to come down. But you do come down. There is a crash, and when you come down you feel a complete mental and physical wreck.

When you are going to crash, you have two alternatives. You can go with the crash and try to get some food and some sleep and eventually feel better. Or you can get more speed right away so you can get high again. When I was doing speed I was taking it enough times to keep me high for three or four days, because I thought I just couldn't take that crash. When you're high for that long a period, the high starts to wear off because of the tolerance you develop. You realize that no matter how much speed you keep taking, you've got to come down.

What happens is that while you're a speed freak, you use all kinds of drugs. You take downs or even marijuana to soften the crash, then speed to get high again. You start mixing ups and downs. After a while, you don't discriminate. You take anything you can get your hands on.

My parents knew that obviously something was wrong. They may have even suspected that I was on drugs. But they never spoke to me about it. There was very little communication between my parents and me at that point. It seems to me that my parents just weren't allowing themselves to think that I might be on drugs. If they did think it, they didn't try to talk to me about it. They were at that time quite ignorant on the subject. After the whole thing finally came out in the open, they learned a lot about drugs, and now we talk about it openly.

I knew that what I was doing was wrong. I knew I really wanted to get off drugs. But the desire for them was so overwhelming that I couldn't help myself. I wasn't physically addicted, but I was certainly psychologically dependent upon it to the point where it soon became the only thing that mattered.

My parents made me see a psychiatrist. My mother got me a regular job at a store where a friend of hers worked. This made my life more structured, but I still had to take speed to be able to function in my job. Going to the psychiatrist didn't get me off speed either, but at least having these two things to do regularly was a start in changing my life style.

After I had saved some money from my job, I suddenly decided to use it to run away. I left New York and went to California. In California I added wine to the list of things I was using. I would smoke a lot of marijuana. I would drink wine. I would occasionally trip. But I was making a conscious effort to get off speed. There were two reasons. One, I realized that I could kill myself with speed. And, two, I was no longer getting the high from speed that I had been getting. I would occasionally do cocaine.

In California I lived in a lot of different places with a lot of different people. At one place there was a girl who talked me into going with her to a place where they had this Yoga course. That was my first experience with Yoga. Much to my surprise, I found right away that it made me feel a lot better than I'd ever felt before.

After about four months in California, my money ran out and I came back home. One of my best friends, who, like me, had been into drugs was now off them. He told me about a Yoga program that had helped him.

I made up my mind that I had to change the way I was living and get off drugs. When my friend told me about the Yoga program at the Horizon Center, something clicked in my mind because of the good experience I had had with Yoga in California. I thought that maybe this was the thing that could change the way I was living. As soon as I came down here I signed up for a class consisting of a very small group of people that met three times a week at night. The class was taught by a man named Guru Prem, who studied Yoga with Swami Satchidananda.

I had no idea how Yoga was going to change me. All I knew from the very beginning was that I wanted to change, and I felt that Yoga could do it.

The actual course consisted of learning a series of postures. Getting into these postures affects certain muscles and glands and gives you a feeling of relaxation. Physical relaxation makes your body feel terrific, and this relieves a lot of mental tension. I got an insight into the fact that a lot of the crazy things I had been doing, a lot of the running to drugs, had been caused by the very same mental tension that I was now able to get rid of through Yoga.

The influence of Guru Prem was also very beneficial. He served as an example for me. He's not an Indian. He's a guy like me, from New York City, whose name, Guru Prem, was given to him by Swami Satchidananda.

The postures are not physical exercises involving straining or sweating. What you do is close your eyes and try to feel your body, by putting your mind into the different parts of your body. The postures then lead into meditation. Whenever the mind starts to wander—and it will, especially at the beginning—you take your mind and put it back on one thing.

There are all sorts of meditations. The kind that I learned is mantra meditation, which consists of using a group of syllables that have certain vibrations when you repeat them over and over again. These vibrations produce an incredible calming effect.

When you first begin learning meditation, you chant the mantra out loud to produce the vibrations. Gradually you chant it lower and lower. Eventually you can produce the vibrations just with lip movements. Finally you can produce the vibrations by merely repeating the mantra mentally.

An example of a very simple mantra would be repeating *Om Shanti*. *Om* is the cosmic syllable of the universe, and *Shanti* means peace. You don't simply repeat the mantra mechanically, but you do it with feeling in order to be able to get to the vibrations. Once I learned meditation I began practicing it, as I do now, twice daily for about ten minutes each time.

Yoga and meditation brought me a discipline I had never had in my life. I saw that I was really responsible for what was happening to me. To be happy and to feel together and to function the way you want to function is not a passive thing. It requires a willingness and an ability to change. Yoga for me has been the tool with which I have been able to bring about the changes in my life that I wanted.

Getting into Yoga is not a quick thing, it's a slow process. It takes a while for your body to loosen up. But what a wonderful feeling it is to feel that you are making progress, especially for someone like myself, who was just drifting. The progress I realized I was making in Yoga made me feel that I was in control of my own life, not being controlled by life. I started to see why I was doing a lot of the things that I was doing. It was because I didn't feel too good about myself.

The desire to get off drugs had started even before I got into Yoga. But it wasn't until I was into Yoga that I was able to get off all drugs. I also stopped doing other negative things, like smoking three packs of cigarettes a day.

I've been into Yoga here about a year now and have been completely free of drugs and tobacco and even wine for over ten months. I am now back at school and doing very well and have already gotten into a college in New Jersey.

TIMMY

The program here showed me there is a better kind of life for me, a life with enjoyment, instead of a life where you always got to put a pistol in your hand to stick somebody up.

Timmy, who started mainlining at thirteen, lives in Washington, D.C., where this interview takes place. Formerly an outpatient at the drug rehabilitation program called Youth Center, he now works there as a counselor.

A product of Washington's slums, he is short, thin, handsome and cheerful. He wears a multi-colored sport shirt, black sharkskin trousers and white sneakers. He moves his hands a lot while he talks.

I'm seventeen now, born and brought up here in downtown Washington, in what we call the poverty area. I live with my father. My mother is dead.

I got into drugs when I was twelve or thirteen years old by trying to be like the older dudes in the neighborhood. I would look up to those fellows of sixteen or seventeen who had the slickest clothes and all the girls. If they used drugs, then I wanted to use drugs. They used drugs.

At about thirteen, I got into this club. The heads of the club were all older and all using drugs—the president, the vice-president, the treasurer and so forth—and to go along with them we younger members started using drugs. We went into heroin right away.

The first thing I did was snorting. I didn't like it, because it made me real drowsy and left me with a nasty taste in my mouth. So, instead of heroin, I started smoking a lot of reefers and drinking wine. But then it got to the point where everybody in the club started using doogie—that's what we called heroin. So I started oiling, which means injecting. I liked oiling better than snorting because it didn't leave a bad taste in my mouth. Once I started, I kept on oiling and oiling and oiling for three years. I had me a good habit.

I was really a needle freak. That means that what I really liked was to stick needles in my arm. It didn't have to be dope, it could be anything. If I couldn't get heroin, I would shoot bam, or barbiturates. Generally, I used to shoot dope five or six times a day. But a lot of times I would just stick a needle in my arm without shooting anything. That's why I say I was a needle freak.

To support my habit, I robbed and stole. Wherever the money was, that's where I was. Stores, dudes, anything and anyone. I used a gun. It's very easy to get a gun in Washington. The first time I used a gun, I borrowed it. It didn't cost me anything. I just said to a friend, "Let me borrow your gun."

He said, "Sure."

There was an understanding that after I robbed a store, I'd give him something. I said, "Thanks, man, for lending me your gun," and I gave him ten dollars. That's how I did it at the beginning, borrowing guns.

But then I found out that our club had its own gun collection. Whenever I wanted to use a gun, I'd just get it from the club. We had all sorts of guns in the club and I could get anything I'd want—rifles, shotguns, pistols, anything. We had this big chest, it was as big as this table, and whenever you wanted a gun you'd just open the chest and pick out any gun you wanted. I used to like this .38 automatic the club had, and that was the gun I used to use all the time, especially for robbing stores.

I got caught robbing stores a number of times. But since I was only fourteen or fifteen, it was easy for me to get released in my father's custody. I had about thirteen charges of armed robbery against me. But I'd never spend more than a few days or a couple of weeks in jail for each charge. But then I got picked up on a charge of attempted murder, and that was more serious.

What happened was that I went into this store and tried to hold up the owner. I was about fifteen at the time, but short for my age and very skinny, because of all the dope I was taking. The owner thought I was playing.

When I said, "Give me all your money!" he just laughed.

He stuck out his hand and said, "Aw, son, you don't want to do that."

I knew there'd be no point in my yelling at him, "Give me the money, I'm not playing!" I knew the only way I could get across to him that I wasn't playing was by shooting him. So I did.

Then he pulled his own gun on me and I had to shoot him again. With all the shooting, the cops came, and that's how I got picked up for attempted murder, even though it turned out the owner wasn't wounded too bad.

I was still a juvenile, so they couldn't sentence me like an adult. The most they could give me was juvenile life, which would mean that I would have to stay locked up until I was twenty-one.

So they locked me up. In jail it was still possible for me to get drugs. They found out that I was on dope, and they had counselors come down to talk to me from the Narcotics Treatment Administration. At first I thought that they couldn't do anything for me, but I would talk to them anyway. They told me about this program they had. I didn't think it could help me, but it was better than being in jail. My lawyer arranged for me to get a suspended sentence and get released into the custody of the Narcotics Treatment Administration.

Once out, I didn't bother coming here at first. I started messing around with drugs right away again, and robbing again. The police got on to me, and just to get them off my back I finally signed up here. But I wasn't sincere about it.

But then once I started going to the therapy sessions, I found I really liked them and became sincere about getting off drugs. At first, what I really liked best about the program was all the different people I was meeting from all the different areas of Washington, and some who had come to Washington from different parts of the country, and even different parts of the world, like Jamaica.

This mixing and being able to communicate with all these different people I really liked. So I would come here every day about twelve o'clock and stay until the place closed, which was ten o'clock in the evening. Then they extended the hours until midnight. This is an outpatient place, so I was able to go home to my father's to sleep.

The first thing they did for me here was to put me on methadone, which made it easy for me to kick heroin.

What helped me the most here was the talking. There were individual sessions with counselors, group therapy, talking to the doctors who came around, and even the administrators and supervisors would always talk to you. There was always somebody to talk to. All this talking wouldn't solve your problems for you, but at least it would give you some kind of ideas to help you solve your problems yourself.

What really appealed to me the most about the program here, what really made an impression on me, was that everybody here was here for only one reason—to help another person, to pull another person up, instead of leaving him down.

I liked the program so much, especially the fact that because of it I wasn't thinking about drugs any more, that I started doing a little volunteer work. Then the administrators offered me a job here.

It was the program here that got me off drugs, because it showed me that there is a better kind of life for me, a life with enjoyment, instead of a life where you always got to put a pistol in your hand to stick somebody up. Because of the program here I was able not only to get off drugs, but to live like a normal human being, to make my own living, and to work five days a week and live for only one thing like everybody else—payday. That's living a life like everybody else, a normal life.

Of course, there is also the work itself, which is satisfying. I'd like to continue in this field as my career, helping people who need help.

Programs such as this one are important, but to get off drugs you have to make up your own mind that it's really what you want to do. Nobody can make you give up drugs except yourself. Somebody could come along and say, "I'm going to spend a hundred million dollars to get you off drugs." But it would be a complete waste of time and money unless you yourself really wanted to get off drugs.

I'm still on methadone, but right now I'm in the process of being detoxified from it. The program here is "detox-abstinence." That means that we aim towards abstinence from all drugs, including methadone, but we use methadone to get off heroin and get us into counseling and group therapy.

Youth Center gives you treatment, real treatment. There's methadone leading to abstinence, there's urine surveillance three times a week, there's individual counseling once or twice a week, and there's group therapy several times a week. And this is very important: there's always somebody around to talk to. Not everybody goes through everything the same here. They try to make the program fit the individual.

We are like one family here. We are all in this together. And everybody has only one purpose here —to help somebody else and in that way help himself.

CLAIRE

You have to want inside to change yourself. Everything I want or need is right here at Synanon. I like it here. It's safe here. It's fun here.

Claire comes from Westwood, a suburb of Los Angeles. She now lives in Santa Monica, California, in the community called Synanon.

Founded in a small apartment by a group of former alcoholics, Synanon now owns a number of houses in California and several other states. "We are not in the business of 'curing' drug addiction," says one of the founders. "Synanon just happens to be a better way for people to live, both with themselves and with others. Here criminals stop committing crimes. Dope addicts stop shooting dope. Whores become ladies. And squares stop taking tranquilizers."

Synanon's headquarters, where Claire lives, are located in a former luxury hotel right on the Pacific Ocean.

Claire is a slender blonde with a small, upturned nose. For the interview she is wearing blue jeans and a Superman T-shirt.

I started with drugs when I was fourteen. Before that, when I was about eleven years old, I began drinking. This was in Westwood, where my parents live. I was born and raised here in California. I've never lived anyplace else.

When I was eleven years old I started going to parties with older guys. There was liquor there, beer and whiskey, and I just started drinking. It was fun. I liked going to these parties much more than I liked being with my parents.

At that time, in fact all the time I was growing up, I was always running away from home. I used to get real drunk on weekends. I didn't go to school very much. Every time I could get out of school I did. I just barely got through junior high school.

When I ran away from home, it was generally for a week and I'd be staying with one of the older guys I'd met at a party.

I had a big problem in the boyfriend area, because no matter what boyfriend I had, my father didn't like him. Even when I was older, well into my teens, my father didn't approve of any of my boyfriends.

My father owns a vending-machine company. My parents were well off and gave me pretty much what I wanted if they were happy with the way I was acting. They treated my younger brother the same way.

I feel my parents did about the best job they could bringing me up. I don't know why I ended up using drugs. I can't push the responsibility off on them. I feel they really loved me, and I think I loved them. I didn't feel that I loved them, though, until I came into Synanon.

Perhaps my parents were too permissive at the beginning. But I don't know if being more strict with me would have helped, because when I wanted to do something, I would just do it. If I didn't want to come home, then I just wouldn't come home.

From eleven to fourteen I was into drinking, and then I began taking barbiturates and smoking grass.

I was in high school at the time. There were a lot of drugs around. Barbiturates and grass were easy to get. They were all over the school. I was still screwing around with older guys, and I got pregnant when I was fifteen.

I didn't like the guy, and he didn't like me, and then I got married to somebody else who wasn't the baby's father. From that time on it was downhill. I gave the baby up for adoption, and left my husband. Then I got pregnant again by another guy, and gave that baby up for adoption, too.

By then I was into LSD, taking it every day. I went from guy to guy, living with a lot of different guys. There was no problem of making a living. The guys would support me.

I was a big disappointment to my parents. They had plans for me to go to college and be in a sorority. Somehow I went the other way, dropping out of school, leaving home, getting knocked up. Twice they thought they were going to have a grandchild. Twice I gave the kid up for adoption. The only time I'd call them was when I needed something.

Finally, I got busted and went to jail for using dope. My parents refused to get me out of jail. One of my friends got me out.

After I got out of jail, I didn't eat. I mean not one bit, for about two weeks. I called up my mother and father and I said, "I'm hungry."

They said, "That's too bad," and they hung up on me.

They just didn't want anything to do with me.

It was after I'd gotten out of the unwed mothers' home and given my second baby for adoption that

I went from using acid to heroin. I just didn't see any future for myself. First I started sniffing, and then I started shooting it in my arms.

I started using so much that I finally moved in with a pusher just to be able to get the stuff. I also got pregnant for the third time, but this time I kept the baby.

We kept getting busted, and I kept getting sick. Every two days I'd get sick, get real sick, and I wouldn't be able to get any money. And plus we moved all around. We were moving about every two months.

Finally, this guy I was living with started working for the police. He became an informer and tipped off the police to all our connections, all the people we knew who sold dope. The police would leave him alone for helping them. They wouldn't bust him, even though they knew he was still a junkie, plus they would even pay him so he could go out and buy dope for the two of us. But since we both had really bad habits by now, the money they paid him wasn't enough and I had to go out and start turning tricks.

I looked so terrible that I could only get as tricks the lowest of the low, I mean creeps who would only pay two dollars. I was five feet five inches tall, but I only weighed ninety pounds. I was sick all the time, plus I had these tracks all up and down my arms, plus I had my son and I was dragging him all over the city. It was awful. I'd go into an apartment with a bunch of creepy guys and walk out with about ten dollars for my old man. He'd take all the money, and I'd still be sick. That's the way it was for quite a long time.

I knew I had to do something. I was afraid the state was going to take my son away.

Finally, my old man double-crossed the cops he

was working for, and now we were in real trouble. Not only were the pushers and junkies he had informed on after us, but so were the cops. We were both really scared now, because we were sure we were going to get killed.

He thought it would be a good idea for us to hide out in Synanon until things cooled down. The plan was for me to come here first and then he would join me later. So I came here to Synanon, but he never showed. He got picked up by the police and is serving a long jail sentence in Carona prison.

When I came here to Synanon, I was really sick. I mean I couldn't get around physically. And, of course, I had to kick cold turkey, because the moment you walk in the door you have to stop using drugs of any kind. I got very sick.

Here's how it works. You just lie upstairs on one of those couches in the living room and people come around and take care of you. They rub your back, you get milk shakes, and they're all nice to you. They talk to you a lot. They ask you about who you are and where you come from. But they don't use any drugs to get you off, no methadone or any of those drugs. You're not even allowed to smoke cigarettes.

There are always people around to talk to you and comfort you all day and even all night. They really help make kicking it a lot easier. It took me about a week to kick cold turkey like that. It wasn't too bad. The only thing was that after that I couldn't sleep at night for about three weeks.

It's funny. I first came here to Synanon because my old man thought it would be a good temporary hideout until things cooled down. He never showed. Instead, he got busted and is still in jail. And I've been here now almost four years.

And I've been off drugs all this time. For three

years I worked in the grade school here. We have our own schools here at Synanon, from nursery school right through high school. And soon we're going to have our own university. I never finished high school, but here I worked as a teacher. Of course, I was studying as well as teaching.

I got my son into Synanon after I was here eight months. He lives in the school now together with the other kids. We have for the kids a kind of kibbutz system, like in Israel.

I worked in the school for about three years and then last month I got a job change into the bakery. I'm learning how to be a baker now.

I liked Synanon right after I got into it for many reasons. First, I had kicked drugs here. Second, there was this feeling of security I got from Synanon. All my life I have had this fear that some policeman would break down my door and put a gun to my head, because that used to happen to me and it scared the hell out of me. Now in Synanon, policemen cannot break in here to take people out.

Then Synanon gave me a job, put me to work, and I liked that. Before I came here, I had never worked a day in my whole life. I thought working was for schmucks. Here I started working and holding down a very responsible job and acting very responsibly in my job.

Another thing I got from Synanon was a husband. I met a guy here when I was here about six months and we fell in love and all that. I've been married to him for a year. That's good.

My kid's in the best school in the whole world, because we don't have any physical violence here. He will never get spanked or pushed or beat up here. Then, like the rest of us, the kids play the Synanon game.

The Synanon game is a situation that's set up for people to talk about how they feel. In the game, you can get mad at somebody. You can yell, and you can tell him to get screwed, or you can tell him anything you want.

Outside the game, you can't tell somebody to get screwed. We act "as if," meaning as if everything was the best it could possibly be. We act polite to each other and courteous and smile and all that. All of our hostility comes out in the Synanon game.

In the game, you feel a lot better after you yell at people. For the game, there's a regular room with twelve chairs in a circle. We sit around and talk to each other, expressing our feelings. Nobody leads the game because there's no leader in the game.

We also have our punishments here, like shaved heads. But that's only for doing something very bad, like smoking or shooting dope or leaving Synanon and then coming back. It's hard to stay at Synanon. It would be much easier to go out and get loaded and kill yourself in about a year, you know. That's an easy life. But to stay here and grow up, develop some character and learn how to be responsible, that's hard.

Some people can't do it. They're cowards. They leave, and when they come back—because they usually come back when they see how bad it is out there —they have to get their heads shaved. Shaving their heads says, "Okay, you can feel bad now, but your hair's going to start growing back."

We have four rules here. Number one, there's no stealing. Number two, no physical violence or the threat of physical violence. Number three, no chemicals, including alcohol. And number four, no smoking. ,

We don't have only ex-addicts here at Synanon.

We have lots of straight people living here who have never had anything to do with drugs but like our life style. These are generally older people who sell their houses and their cars and move into Synanon. They live here and eat here and sleep here and play the Synanon game here, but they work outside. Many of them have their own businesses outside, which is fine, because they donate all their profits to Synanon.

The younger people would rather not work outside. They would rather work for somebody in Synanon, because then they can play the Synanon game with their boss, and say anything they want to him. They don't have to tolerate a lot of bullshit that goes on out there at a regular job.

Working on the outside may be all right for the older people with their own businesses. But for the rest of us, the real Synanon people, especially those of us who were into drugs, I think we've got to be completely connected to Synanon for the rest of our lives. I believe that if I ever left Synanon, I would start using drugs again.

The Synanon game is the heart of the therapy here at Synanon. Around here everything is public. Everybody knows what everybody does. Everything is talked about very openly. My relationship with my husband is better than any I ever had because it's public, and because I can play the Synanon game with him.

If you're not married, you can still have a good relationship here at Synanon, including sex. If you're single and you want sex with someone, you can use what we call the Guest Room. You have to book it in advance, but you can spend the whole night there with another person. You can even book it for three nights a week or even five nights a week.

Of course, you have to get permission to have

sexual relations here at Synanon. You even have to get permission, if you're involved with someone, to be able to hold hands in public. And you have to be at least eighteen years old to get permission for sexual relations.

My husband and I used the Guest Room for a whole year before we got married. It's not hard to get permission for sex or to use the Guest Room if you're not married. Sex outside of marriage is encouraged here at Synanon, because it's healthy and a very natural thing.

Synanon can not only get you off drugs, but lead you to a whole better way of life for yourself. But you have to want inside to change yourself and get yourself in constant motion. You've got to want to grow up and want to go through some changes at Synanon.

We look at it like this. You stop using drugs as soon as you come into Synanon. Hopefully, at Synanon, you'll learn how to develop some character. Your life style is just a tool to do that.

I like these people at Synanon. Even if I weren't a dope fiend, I would want to live here because I like the people here. I like Synanon. Everything I want or need is right here at Synanon. I like it here. It's safe here. It's fun here.

GEORGE

Having time to think things out for myself was the kind of therapy that really worked for me. Just sitting and being alone, even in a locked cell, had a great deal to do with it.

George, who comes from Harlem, started sniffing heroin at the age of fifteen. Now, at nineteen, he is being treated for heroin addiction under a New York State program.

His eyes are quick, his mind is quick, and he has a quick, ready smile. He wears a black leather jacket, dungarees and sneakers.

(At the time of the interview George was concerned about passing his high-school equivalency test and being admitted to college. Recently he learned that he had succeeded in both.)

Well, it all began when I was fifteen years old. At that time, for my age I was running kind of wild. I wanted freedom. I didn't want my mother to be on my back all the time. I didn't want my sisters to be on my back all the time.

Every time I would stay out it was, like, "Where you been?" and "What you been doing?" And I kept hearing this from my sisters and my mother. My sisters, I guess they were trying to be, like, helpful with me because they knew the hell that my mother was going through with me plus the fact that she and my father had just separated.

I was rebellious. I wanted to find things out on my own, because I felt like that was the only way I was to learn. But the constant pressure from my mother and my sisters and the school I was going to was just the opposite. They all wanted me to do what they wanted me to do, not what I wanted me to do.

I was hurt just looking at my mother, knowing the pain caused by the separation and the hell that she was going through. And I felt for this, and this is what made me not actually try to hurt her physically. My father? Yeah, well, I could knock him out anytime I wanted to, whenever he pushed me. But my mother, I don't care how mad I got at her, it was just something I couldn't do. Why? Because she was my mother and I respected her, even though she did get on my nerves.

Then there were the pressures at school. My marks in school went down. I got suspended for not going to classes. To get away from it all—the problems at home and the problems at school—I took to drugs.

I just said one day, "Fuck it," and I went out there to snick me a bag. It was easily available in my neighborhood. Before all this pressure on me I never thought of using drugs. I would point my nose the other way. But you know, this tension that was constantly building up on me made me finally just say, "I'm going to do it."

I started by sniffing heroin, and I did that a good eight months.

At first it was at a slow pace, I guess about one bag on the weekend. And then it started growing higher and higher, three, four times a day.

I liked it because it got me away from all my problems. It's that feeling like, you know, you don't give a fuck. You just lay back and relax and enjoy yourself.

What I disliked about it was that once you didn't have the money, you had to go hustle and bum. And this, you know, in the beginning made me feel like, "Damn, I'm beginning to look like one of these bums out here on the street and I don't want to be looking like that." But you did it anyway, because you wanted that bag and nothing could keep you from chasing that blue bag out there in the wilderness.

At first my mother was giving me the money I needed for drugs. Then off and on I got jobs here and there. Of course, my mother didn't know I was buying drugs with the money she was giving me. She just asked me why I spent so much money so fast. I'd say, "Well, prices on everything are going up higher and higher all the time." I'd shrug it off as best I could.

It was costing me a good ten dollars a day just for drugs. When I didn't get enough money from my mother I'd steal. I'd steal money from my house. I also took to snatching pocketbooks. I never got caught. I never got busted.

I also never got to the point where I was sick as a dog. But I could tell that I was getting there because I wasn't eating. I started losing weight. That's when my mother started noticing things and found out I was on drugs. If she hadn't decided to do something about it immediately and sign me into some sort of program, I probably would still be out there.

At first my mother tried to get me into a private treatment center. I lived there two weeks, but I didn't like that type of therapy. The first thing I didn't like was they didn't want no mustache. They figured I was the image of a drug addict. Also, I was still taking drugs all the time I was at the center, still getting high.

When I first got there, I didn't want to talk about my social problems, such as problems with my mother. I didn't feel like I could trust them with that just then and there. I'm very careful about, you know, whose hands I'll put my emotions in. I don't like to be hurt.

But this is what I was trying to avoid from them, all that yelling and screaming at the encounter sessions. I mean, you don't talk to nobody by screaming at them. You just don't talk to nobody like that—no human being. If you expect somebody to listen to you, I think there's a certain way of how you talk to that person to make him understand.

After two weeks at that private center, I split and went back to the street. When I got into the New York State program, I met people who had been to that center and had come out and fucked up. They were begging to go back to the center. Why? Because they was crying, "I need help, I need help."

To me it seemed like they were leaning on the center with their type of therapy. I don't think it should be that way.

Anyway, after I split from the center, my mother took me down to Family Court. They told her what to do to get me into the New York State program, and she went and got the papers, and that was that. I had to go to court or else they would have put a warrant out on me.

My first stop was a State residential center in Greenwich Village. I was there only five days. Then they cut me loose from there. Instant aftercare! I said, "God damn!"

You know why they did that? Because the place was overcrowded. So they just turned me out in the street after I just got in. I couldn't understand it, but I was glad to leave. I had brainwashed myself into the idea that I was cured. So I went back out there— the streets.

I didn't know I was really kidding myself. I was just so glad to get the hell out of there, and enjoy some of that nice weather, that it just never dawned on me that I was going back on drugs. Within a few weeks I had a habit, and I started stealing some money from my brother, and I started selling my clothes. I didn't want to go to school. And I never reported to the State Narcotics Commission officer like I was supposed to. I didn't report for a month.

Then, suddenly, one day I decided I better start reporting. This was after I stole some money.

I ran off my mouth that time. I wasn't bullshitting. I was beginning to think about myself at the time.

They put me into this therapeutic class. But I was still fucking up. And the people at the Narcotics Commission found out about it because my mother and sister kept calling them: "You got to do something. . . . I'm getting cards from school saying he wasn't in school. . . . I'm missing some money."

I was up in therapy, trying to convince myself that there's still a hope—when Smithy, my State counselor, calls me down to his office and tells me I got to go back to the residential center in Greenwich Village. So I told him, "I'm not going to give you a hard time. I'll go back there."

I figured I'm going there for only fourteen days. But I spend a month there. Then I'm being shipped out to Woodbourne, a maximum security place upstate. I could tell you a book about that place. Let me tell you, you don't play with them people up there. You get your head knocked in. I mean, these people carry blackjacks—no guns, but lots of big sticks.

The joint, I feel, did a hell of a lot of good for me. I was in a cell by myself for four months. And this constant thinking is making me aware of what's really right for me.

I had the type of counselor there who was a very understanding guy. He would know the bullshit lines because he had heard them many times before. So you're not putting nothing over on nobody but yourself if you tried it with him. But that man never let you make him your crutch. He'd say, "You can tell me anything you want to tell me, but I won't be around you forever."

He told me I had some pretty constructive ideas about what I was going to do, and all I had to do was just apply them. He helped give me peace of mind with myself.

But mainly what Woodbourne did for me was to give me time to think about what I wanted to do. Having time to think things out for myself was the kind of therapy that really worked with me. Just sitting and being alone, even in a locked cell, had a great deal to do with it. There nobody put any thoughts in my mind except myself.

I figured like this: That was the first time I was

ever locked behind a cell door. And I didn't dig the idea. I didn't like the position that I was in. I had this small two-by-four room and this bed that wouldn't even fit me and I'm small. Then there were the horse-hairs getting in your back, you know? Yeah, they didn't even give you a mattress in the cell. All that put a scar on my brain that I would never forget. I'll never forget that experience.

This is what made me decide, "George, you got to do something." This being alone was what helped me —no group therapy, only my type of therapy, my mental therapy.

You see, I can't speak for some other person because I don't have the feelings and emotions of another person. All I know is how I beat it, which is through isolation. *Isolation within myself.* It's true, I was isolated within a facility, but I was isolated in myself. And it was only this isolation within myself that brought out my idea of what I want to do for myself.

I want to have a decent home, to have what most people want. I want to be average. I want to have money, to be able to go riding around in a car, to be financially secure.

When I first got out of Woodbourne, which was seven months ago, my plan was to get a job in a bank and go to night school. But I found out that banks don't want you if you don't have a high-school diploma or at least high-school equivalency. And even with the high-school diploma, there's a lot of people who want bank jobs. So I started thinking.

Meanwhile Smithy, my old counselor, tells me they're giving the high-school equivalency in November. So for two months now I've been coming to day care here in the city every day, studying, applying myself. I've gotten to know just about everybody in the day-care building. They liked what I was doing, they saw that I was really applying myself.

But, you know, they weren't really patting me on my back because they know how it is for a person to be patted on their back—they revert right back to that bag that they was in. I didn't want to be patted on the back. Just by trying, I haven't achieved anything yet. But I feel that everything that I want to do is beginning to happen. And I think if you have patience and you don't get discouraged, and if you stick to your main objective of what you want to do, you'll make it.

My main goal now is to get into a college out on Long Island. I put down that I'd like to major in business administration. I don't know if I'll stick with it. I think I may instead go in for teaching. I really dig social studies. History is my thing. I'm very interested in it.

I don't know. I'll just have to see when I get into college.

For about six years I'd been a heavy drug user. I got out of drugs completely on my own. However, once I was off drugs, I did get into a wonderful program to help me stay off drugs.

Mitchell, who comes from Far Rockaway, New York, is of medium height, slim, with blond hair and blue eyes. During the interview at Roosevelt Hospital in Manhattan, he speaks quickly, but softly, gently. He looks the interviewer straight in the eye, and he has an air of warmth and openness that is most appealing.

Although legally considered blind, Mitchell can see something clearly if he holds it very close to his eyes. He is wearing a tan suede suit. "Since I can't drive," he says, "I put money I might have put into a car into clothes."

I got into drugs, I guess, because of problems in my house—because of things that happened to me like, you know, the way I felt about myself. I was a very, very skinny, ugly little kid.

And it made me feel even worse that the only kids I could hang out with, that would accept me, were the kids who did crazy wild things—like taking drugs. So you can say I started fooling around with drugs in Far Rockaway when I was about ten. I started by sniffing glue.

For five years I went to a Jewish religious school, a yeshiva. It was an all-boys school. And this was the terrible thing, combined with the fact that my mother would never let me out of the house. My parents were strict, treating me like a prisoner. I had no friends except two Jewish friends my mother let me play with in the last year I was there. Then when I was nine these two kids moved away to Long Island and I had no friends at all. I played the whole year by myself in the yard.

Being alone so much was bad for me. It made me afraid of people. I could never talk to them. And then when I got into a public school with girls, it got even worse. That's when I started hanging around with the crazy kids.

They were Jewish, Catholic, Irish, Italian, white, black. They accepted me because I always had money. I was the one to buy things most of the time. I always had bread—bread to buy glue.

I started with the glue when I was ten. I started with about one, two tubes a day and I got up to about eight. When I got into junior high school, I was absent a hundred and thirty-eight days my first year there. I never thought I was going to be promoted, but I got promoted.

I used to squeeze the tube into a paper bag and

sniff it through my nose or mouth, whichever was clearer. I got high either way, usually ending up with glue all over my face and hands. It was terrible, but I didn't care because of the dreams.

The day I stopped sniffing glue, I had a dream I still remember. I was sitting in a rocking chair in our basement, which was filled with furniture, and I was sniffing. Suddenly, underneath one of the chests of drawers I saw a rag. I said, "That looks like a ghost," and I felt very sorry for it. I said, "Gee, I'd really like to help this ghost if I could."

And then from the end of the floor, where the wall was, a luminous green net started to come towards me. It came all the way over my head, and it touched my hand, and the whole thing disappeared except for a piece in my hand. I said, "Wow, I gotta save this or people'll never believe it." And then the piece in my hand disappeared.

I got mad and said, "Ha, ha, ha, I wouldn't help that ghost if I could." And suddenly, in the floorboards, needles appeared and they started shooting at me, one at a time. I picked my feet up off the floor and let the needles all shoot past me.

And then I did it again and I said, "Ha, ha, ha, I wouldn't help that ghost if I could." Then a round water boiler we have started coming towards me, and I got really scared and I hid my eyes and I said, "Go away. I won't do it no more."

But then I did it one more time. I said, "Ha, ha, ha, I wouldn't help that ghost if I could." No sooner were the words out of my mouth when a big cup appeared on top of the boiler, and I knew what was going to happen. The cup was going to try to suffocate me.

I tried to hide between the furniture and said, "I'll never sniff glue again as long as I live." And I opened my eyes and everything was gone. The glue had worn off.

I swore I'd never sniff glue again. But that night I did it again, and my mother caught me. She threatened to take me to the Board of Health unless I quit. After that I quit glue for good.

I quit not only because I promised my mother I would, but because I myself realized it wasn't good for me. I didn't feel good and I was in bad physical shape too. By the time I was thirteen I was about the same height I am now—five feet, eight inches. But I weighed only a hundred and two pounds. That's what sniffing glue for three years had done for me. So my mother catching me and threatening to turn me over to the Board of Health clinched it for me. I promised her I'd quit, and I did quit—cold! But almost immediately afterwards I started getting into other things.

First there was drinking. Me and my friends, we drank together. We were all too young to go into a liquor store, so we'd get an old bum to buy it for us and we'd give him a quarter. We would drink whatever we could get hold of—beer, wine, hard liquor, anything. We'd go under the boardwalks and just try to get stoned, but I'd always get sick.

Then I started smoking pot. The first time I ever smoked pot was on the beach. A couple of friends of mine gave me a joint.

Then I went away for the summer. As soon as I came back, I went over to a friend's house and we split up a bag between three of us and had about six or eight joints apiece. Then, for the first time, I got stoned, really stoned, on pot.

But after a while I began to hate pot and I just couldn't smoke it, because it made me feel effeminate. I couldn't stand the way I swished when I walked. Especially with the two friends I smoked with, because they were very masculine, and it seemed that the more that I swished, the more masculine they got. I couldn't stand it, so I cut down on pot and I would only smoke it if there was nothing else around to be had.

Well, from then on I went into just about everything except heroin. I guess one of the reasons I felt this big need for drugs was because I had a big hang-up about chicks. I was so skinny and ugly, no girl would go for me. Even if we were in a group where there was an extra girl, she wouldn't go for me. She'd go over to somebody else even if he already had a girl, and hang around with the two of them rather than be alone with me.

After pot, I went into cough medicine. Then I used to do snappers. They're little orange capsules which increase the heartbeat for people with bad hearts.

And I used to do stuff called Rinalgin, which is a nasal spray. But you can't buy that at all any more. It's off the market completely. You could stay up all night long on Rinalgin and all you did was talk, but it was beautiful. The next morning you felt shitty, but all night long you felt terrific.

Then when I was about fifteen and a half I started taking acid.

My parents found out that after I stopped sniffing glue, I was taking other drugs. My father tried to stop me by beating the shit out of me.

Another thing I didn't like about being on drugs was some of the things I did to get money to buy drugs. There are a few things that I did while on drugs that I'm really ashamed of, things I never even brought out in group therapy. This is the first time I've ever talked to anybody about them.

One of the things that I did was when I was fifteen years old. I met this retarded girl on the train who was coming back from a special school in Manhattan and talked to her for a while and weaseled my way into getting her to take me home. Once I got in the house, I started fooling around and she really didn't know what was going on. She was very much out of it, in her own little world.

I cleaned out the whole house. I took a gold charm bracelet with four gold coins. I don't know whether it was hers or her mother's. I took a brass microscope, a twenty-one-carat gold watch and another watch, a couple of bottles of champagne, and about a hundred dollars in cash.

I also took a house key because I was going to go back to clean the place out. This girl's father was a doctor, and I figured I could get a lot of good stuff in there if I came back. But that plan fizzled out because I lost my nerve.

The bracelet and the gold coins I sold for a hundred and twenty-five dollars. The watches brought only three dollars at school. The microscope I gave away to a friend.

Another thing I did that I'm very ashamed of was the time I stole the public-address system out of a Catholic church in Far Rockaway. I sold it to a band for fifteen or twenty bucks.

One Saturday night, I dropped some acid and I was smoking some grass and I was really stoned out of my mind. I went to Far Rockaway, and I got into a fight, and I got kicked in the head a few times.

About five days later I was blind. And then about three days after that I lost the use of my left side, became completely paralyzed. I couldn't walk. In the hospital they gave me all the tests.

After two weeks of tests they were going to send

me home blind, claiming there was nothing they could do for me. Then they tried cortisone, which they at first had been hesitant to give me because I had a bad stomach. The cortisone treatments began to bring my vision back, and they released me.

For about half a year my vision kept getting better until it stopped at the point it is now. I can't drive or anything, but I can get around. The only thing I really can't do is drive. Like, I go skiing. And real close up I see pretty good.

They never found out exactly what it was that blinded me. They say that it may have been a combination of all the years I was taking drugs and the kicks in the head that did something to my nervous system. Also, the grass I smoked that night had been ground up in an old pepper mill, and they said that maybe the grass got contaminated by some very old pepper that had turned poisonous.

Anyway, as my eyesight began to come back, the use of my left side came back too. After two months in the hospital, I was released.

At about the age of sixteen, I began working for my father, because I couldn't go back to school. My vision wasn't good enough to see the blackboard. And then I got into the Division of Vocational Rehabilitation. They sent me to the art school that I'm going to now. I've been there for about two years.

Even with my bad eyesight, I've been studying book and magazine illustration. I've always been good with art, and they taught me what I didn't know. I'm entered in a contest right now sponsored by the Society of Illustrators, for a five-hundred-dollar prize.

Getting blinded was what cured me of taking drugs. I've been clean from the time I got out of the hospital till now. That's about five years.

Once off drugs I began to gain weight. In a matter of months I gained fifty pounds, which brought me up to my present weight of about a hundred and forty-five.

I saw that I didn't need drugs. I had taken them because that was the only thing I could do to be with people. And when I saw that I didn't need to take drugs to be with people, I stopped.

For about six years I'd been a heavy drug user—everything but heroin. I'd even been injecting myself with liquid amphetamines.

I quit cold because I got scared after I got blinded. But I got out of drugs completely on my own. I had no help whatsoever. However, once I was off drugs, I did get into a wonderful program at Roosevelt Hospital to help me stay off drugs. A friend of mine was in this program where kids first tried to resolve their problems and then get off drugs. I did it backwards. I got off drugs, but I still had all the problems that brought me to drugs. I'd never resolved them, my problems, even though I'd stopped taking drugs.

Between the time I was fourteen and sixteen, I never talked to my father at all, not about anything. The only time I would talk to him was when he would come home from work and if my mother had had a fight with me, she'd tell him about it. He'd yell at me and chase me out of the house and I'd sleep on the beach with a bottle of wine. But that was the only time I talked to him during those two years.

My mother had never let me be a normal kid. Where all the kids would go out in the street in the summer under the fire hydrant, I was never allowed to because my mother didn't want me to get wet.

All this I came to realize only after I got into the Roosevelt Hospital program. You see, after I stopped taking drugs, I was still feeling terrible inside. I still couldn't relate to people; I couldn't talk to anybody; I couldn't meet a girl. I was scared. I couldn't look at anybody squarely; I had to look down at the floor. I was, after a couple of years, to the point where I was beginning to think of going back to drugs. It was then that this friend of mine told me about the program at Roosevelt Hospital. Through him I joined the group run by Irwin Levine.

I saw that good things could happen to me if I really began to open myself up. Now I can talk to people, and I really want to try to help people. I definitely don't want to see anything happen to anyone like what happened to me. I never felt this way before. Before it was always all me.

The group has helped me a hundred percent since I've been there by bringing out of me the things that I had pent up, by making me admit to things, by making me see things the way they really are instead of looking at them the way I fantasized. And by making me realize that I'm not unique and that there are other people who have the same problems that I have, the same difficulties that I had.

The group-encounter sessions at Roosevelt Hospital changed my life for the better. A lot of the credit goes to Irwin Levine. He's an ex-addict himself, and he can help you better than any psychiatrist.

Without Irwin's group I don't know whether I would have stayed off drugs. I began to relate to people. I got to know a little bit about myself. I also began to grow. They give you a little bit of responsibility by asking you to help out in certain ways and asking you to do things. This makes you feel good.

And this social thing definitely carries over outside the group. People that I couldn't talk to, wouldn't even look at, I can tell them to go fuck themselves now. I mean the ones I don't like. The ones I like, I can tell them I like them, but not as much as I'd like to at this point. I still got a lot to learn.

I've been off drugs now five years and I can't see myself ever going back to them. I know socially I still have far to go, but I also know I've made a lot of progress.

I've got a blind date tomorrow night with someone I've never met who's supposed to be nice, and I'm hoping it's going to work out.

MARIO

I got started on drugs when I was in Vietnam. With just straight psychiatric care, I'd get more hooked than ever. But with methadone and group therapy I'd say the results have been excellent.

Mario, who comes from Queens, New York, enlisted in the Navy as a medical corpsman at the age of eighteen. He was sent to serve with the Marines in Vietnam, where he got hooked on heroin.

He is now an outpatient at a Veterans Administration hospital, where the interview takes place. He is a good talker and loves to act out what he is talking about. While describing his career as a "cattle rustler," for example, he demonstrates how to do it through skillful pantomime.

I got started on drugs when I was a medical corpsman with the Marines in Vietnam. I was with the first group of Marines that was over there. We had it pretty rough. The job that I had wasn't such a good job. I did four months in graves registration, embalming people. That kind of got me. Four months of that, I think, would get anybody—cleaning up the dead and sending them to Texas. They used to dress them in Texas. After a few months of embalming duty, I'd have combat duty.

I started with morphine. I had a lot of morphine Syrettes, and I used to inject myself with them. I had to be stoned to go out in the field, because I'd never know if I was coming back.

I'd go out there in case anybody needed medical assistance, but I was only allowed to carry a .45. And what good was that going to do me unless the guy was on top of me? And being a corpsman, I was an easy target for the enemy.

I needed something to get me by. I tried drinking, but I just couldn't get that cheap hooch down. They were making their own stuff over there. So I started messing around with my own morphine Syrettes. I found that that did something to me.

But after a while, I couldn't use morphine any more because my Chief Petty Officer was getting wise to a few other guys on morphine, and I didn't want him to get wise to me. So I stopped. But when I stopped, I felt funny. I was sick.

So this other corpsman said, "Listen, come with me." And one night we went into Saigon. We picked up some prostitutes in an alley who introduced us to this connection. From then on I made it on my own with heroin. I met different connections here and there—in barbershops, among other places. No matter where you went, you could find heroin.

It was very cheap. A pack of cigarettes got three days' supply of heroin, a carton of cigarettes maybe a month's supply. What you get over here for a thousand dollars you can get in Vietnam for thirty.

When I got out of Vietnam I cleaned up, because I still had two years to go in the Navy. I had sea duty on board a destroyer in the Mediterranean fleet. I didn't touch any drugs all that time. I kept clean.

Three months before I got out of the Navy, my ship was in the Navy yard down in Portsmouth, Virginia, and I was coming home on weekends. I found the guys I grew up with in my neighborhood were into heroin. This was in Queens, in a middle-class neighborhood, predominantly white.

These friends of mine started showing off, saying to me, "Look, we're on heroin." I told them that I was into heroin two years ago when I was in Vietnam and I didn't want to do it any more. You see, I knew I could get hooked on it. I was still in the service and I wanted to get out with an honorable discharge. I didn't want to mess up with only three months to go.

What finally happened was that my father got very sick. He was dying in the hospital. Things started building up around me. I knew that when I got out of the Navy I was going to have to carry the load at home. All these pressures got me back on heroin.

I guess I really wanted to get back on it. I was lying to myself, saying the reason was my father's sickness. I needed an excuse and this was the easiest excuse I could use to go back to heroin.

I started snorting it at first, but I didn't get the same effect as I did when I had mainlined it over in Vietnam. I remembered having a better head mainlining. So I went into mainlining every weekend when I came home. Finally, I got out of the service and then I went right into heavy mainlining.

I came to this hospital three times to try to kick before they had this program. Before, I was in the psychiatric ward. Each time, I left the hospital with a worse habit than I had when I came in because heroin was so easy to get in this hospital.

After the third time I had tried to kick it in the psychiatric ward, I got out and was really in bad shape. Instead of going back home, I took to the streets. For three weeks my home was an old abandoned car. Sometimes I'd sleep on a filthy mattress on a rooftop.

I supported my habit by becoming a "cattle rustler." That's our name for somebody who steals meat from supermarkets and sells it at half-price. Me and three other guys, we had this kind of team.

I'd take the meat from the racks and put it right down my pants. When I'd get undressed at night my underwear would have as much blood on it as a woman who was having that time of the month. My underpants would be saturated with blood.

I never got caught. Veal cutlets, however, were dangerous to steal. They would bleed like a son of a gun and you'd be walking through the store and the blood would be running out your pants all over the place.

After a couple of months I got tired of living on the streets and being a cattle rustler. I was fed up and I wanted to come home. My mother said, "What are you going to do, come home again and do the same thing over? Clean up for a few days?" She said, "I'll tell you what. You come home for a few days. You clean up. But as soon as you mess up again, we're committing you into the New York State program." She had the papers already drawn up.

Then one of my friends told me about this new program they were starting in the V.A. hospital. I told my mother about it, but she didn't like the idea. "No," she said, "not the V.A. hospital again. You were there three times before, and those psychiatrists didn't do anything for you."

But then I told her that this program was going to be different, that it wasn't psychiatrists but with methadone.

She said, "Let's look into it."

So we looked into it, and I got on it.

It's terrific. I've been on it six months and I haven't taken heroin once. In addition to the methadone, I get psychotherapy, mainly group therapy, once a week. Together with methadone, psychotherapy is very good, because kicking cold turkey is a lot of stress. It's impossible to maintain yourself and go to group therapy while you're kicking. When you're taking methadone, it eliminates all the stress. You can rap and talk with your mind at ease.

If you're a nervous wreck, it's no good talking. It only gets you more upset. This is what used to happen to me when I was in the psychiatric ward. We would rap, but I was going through cold turkey at the time, and I'd just get more and more aggravated. After the rap session was over, we were allowed to go anywhere in the hospital. First thing I'd do was find a dealer here. Then I'd shoot up and go back to the psychiatric ward all bright-eyed and bushy-tailed.

With just straight psychiatric care, I'd get more hooked than ever. But with methadone and group therapy, I'd say the results, at least with me and a lot of the other guys here, have been excellent.

I come here now as an outpatient. I'm back living with my family in Queens. Next week I start work as a social-service worker here in the hospital. Everything is fine.

GLORIA

I couldn't see how I could live without the drugs. I was hunting for peace. I found it, the happiness, the joy, the completeness. The Lord has come into my life.

Gloria is tall, good-looking and very bright. She comes from Uniontown, Pennsylvania, about forty miles south of Pittsburgh. Of Polish descent, the daughter of a coal-mine superintendent, she was head nurse of a Pittsburgh hospital by the age of twenty-one. But the drugs she had started using as a teenage student nurse forced her out of nursing into a life of prostitution, shoplifting and serious illness.

Gloria now works with an organization called Teen Challenge, which has drug-treatment centers in almost every state in the country. Gloria's interview takes place at the Teen Challenge center in Rhinebeck, New York. Located on a former estate, it has spacious, wooded grounds and comfortable live-in quarters.

I come from a very average middle-class family. My father is superintendent of a coal mine. And my mother off and on during the years worked as a secretary in a hospital. My family was interested in giving me all the material things that they never had, because both of them had grown up during the Depression.

On the surface it seemed that we were the ideal family. Actually, we were just putting on a show when neighbors were around. But after the neighbors or my friends had gone home, that great emptiness in our lives was there. None of us was really happy. We only pretended to be. We were hypocrites and phonies—even my twin brother and sister, who are two years younger than I.

My father was seeing another woman on the side. And because my mother knew about it, she and my father used to have big battles at home in front of my brother and sister and myself.

I was brought up in the Russian Orthodox Church, very strict. We fasted. We kept the holy days. We never did anything on Sundays except go to church. It really didn't mean anything to any of us. But my mom insisted we keep going in order to show the neighbors we were a perfect family, a churchgoing family.

The most disturbing thing, though, for my brother and sister and myself, when we were growing up, was this other woman. There was always the question of divorce, and there was this constant battle about whether they were going to get the divorce or whether they weren't going to get the divorce. And we kids were dragged into it by being asked to make choices: If we get divorced, will you stay with your mother or do you want to go with your father? But they never did get divorced or even separated.

My father finally gave up his girlfriend, but my mother never let him forget it.

I was never close to my father or my mother. I grew up with the idea that I just wasn't good enough, and that to please them, to get their love, I had to be exceptional, to be perfect. But I couldn't be that way. I always felt rejected. I know that a lot of those feelings of rejection were only my imagination. But I didn't see that until years later.

In high school, I found myself in a crowd of kids that were smoking cigarettes and drinking a lot. And I said, "Well, here I am. I don't enjoy any of this. I'm being a phony just like my parents." So I just kind of dropped all my school friends and kept to myself. I became very introspective. I read a lot.

After I graduated from high school, I stopped going to church. I told my mother I didn't want anything more to do with religion. I decided I wanted to be a nurse. I needed something where people would love me or at least really need me.

So I went into nurse's training and the first two years were really exciting. It was new, the people were new, it was a respected profession, the studies were fascinating, and I really loved it.

Then I met a guy and we got engaged and everything was really beautiful for a while. But then I began to see things in him. I saw that we really had the same kind of relationship that my mother and father had. I was the one making all the decisions.

That's how it had been with my parents. My mother was the one who decided what restaurants to eat at, where to go on vacations, what kind of car we should have. She even controlled the money. Aside from that woman my father had for a while, she was in charge of everything. And when I found myself acting like my mother, bossing my fiancé around all over the place, I broke the engagement.

I was at nursing school in Pittsburgh when I broke off this relationship. The breakup gave me a really bad depression. This is where I started picking up with the drugs.

In nursing school, the drugs were easy to get. I started with Benzedrine to help me study, to stay awake nights to study. And then diet pills to get me that extra lift through the day, and sleeping pills at night. A lot of the nursing students took pills. So did the interns and medical students.

I never became hooked on them. They were just something to get me through the day and help me sleep at night. I learned to depend on chemicals.

I got an apartment by myself. I could afford it. I was now a registered nurse at the hospital. I was doing well at my work, but there was still this emptiness inside of me. It was like I was dead inside. The eight hours a day at the hospital, helping sick people, were fine. But I still had sixteen other hours to get through.

As for my social life, I'd go out with people, but I really wouldn't enjoy them. So then maybe for the next couple of weeks I'd just stay by myself.

There were a couple of bars in Pittsburgh where the hippie kids used to hang out. I went over there, and I met some kids who had dropped out. They were playing at being writers or artists or musicians. Some of them were street people. For a while I began to feel like I really could belong there. I was grateful that these people accepted me.

Among the hippie crowd I met a guy, a painter, who was also living a double life. He had been through college and was teaching art in a settlement house. My new boyfriend was married and I didn't see him too much—just on weekends and sometimes during the week. He was in his thirties and had two children, and I was about nineteen.

Anyway, he was the one who turned me on to marijuana, and I smoked a lot of it after work. He'd buy it for me and he'd leave it with me. I learned how to roll it up by myself, and I'd just smoke the whole evening long until he could come over or until I could see him.

And then I noticed something strange about him. Friday nights he'd disappear. I'd never know where he was or, like, maybe he'd say he was coming over but then I didn't see him.

Finally he told me that he had been messing around with heroin. He said he didn't have a habit, that he was only doing it on weekends. He also said he wanted me to help him get off of it. I found out I couldn't, and then I began to get curious. I figured, "What could be so powerful to take him away from me? There must be something to it." So within a couple of months he gave in and let me try heroin.

Before I started using heroin I was messing around with LSD, but I never liked that too much. Every one of my trips was bad. I saw terrible things. I saw my face melting in the mirror, and I just looked so ugly and so horrible to myself, and I was filthy, filthy dirty. And I was always afraid of what was going to happen to me. The last trip I took I sat in one place and didn't say anything for eight hours. It was terrible. So I didn't want any more of that.

So this one shot of heroin was just to find out what it was like. I figured, "Well, I know all about it. I know what it does. I see junkies come in. I take care of them in the hospital." We always had one bed for junkies, and they used to talk to me and tell me what it was like.

I knew it all. I never thought it could happen to me.

I'll never forget that first time. It was in my apartment, in the kitchen. I can remember, oh, for hours and hours I was high. I was doing all the things I'd been wanting to do. On heroin, you feel you can do anything you want and be anything you want, and solutions to all your problems are right there during the time you're high.

Heroin is a depressant. It depresses the brain, the central nervous system, and relaxes you completely. This first time I got sick and vomited, but it wasn't a sick feeling. Even the vomiting was pleasurable, if you can understand that.

We decided that it would be a weekend thing with me, too. But it progressed from the weekend to the middle of the week and then to Monday. Pretty soon it was every day. And before I knew it I had a habit. The money I was earning as a nurse I gave to my boyfriend so he could buy the dope for himself and for me.

Then I got hepatitis—from using a dirty needle. Even though I was a nurse and knew all about sterilization, especially the importance of sterilizing hypodermic needles, I didn't care. I was just so anxious to get the drug inside me.

So I got hepatitis and I ended up in the hospital for a month, and I stayed off the drugs for that month. It wasn't hard to get off that first time. As for withdrawal symptoms, I was a little uncomfortable, but that was all. And once I came out of the hospital, I started right back again. Only this time it was worse. I got greedy and I started using more and more and more and more. I went from one bag to maybe five bags a day.

It was getting expensive, but I had a larger salary now, because I had become head nurse of the hospital. My boyfriend couldn't give too much money because of having to support his family. So I was doing most of the paying for our habit.

Then I began going around to doctors, doing what they call "making doctors." These are essentially crooked doctors. You can go to them every day, and as long as you pay one way or another they give you a prescription. I was getting Dilaudid on prescription. Dilaudid is a synthetic opium derivative, and it did the trick pretty much; it got you high. The crooked doctors would generally charge twenty dollars for the first visit, and then after that six dollars for every prescription they wrote. Since these prescriptions were not renewable, I had to go to these doctors every day. Every day.

Finally, I got hepatitis again. I had a really bad case this time and required intravenous feeding. But I continued to take my heroin through the I.V. tube! Whenever my boyfriend visited me he'd bring me the heroin. Nobody suspected anything. It was pretty cool.

After I got out of the hospital, I found myself using even more drugs. After a time I saw the habit was getting real expensive, and I was getting tired of it. It wasn't even worth it any more. So I started making the rounds of psychiatrists. But each time I'd drop the therapy. When they started questioning me and it got so that it was getting painful and I didn't feel that I could take it any more, I'd go back to drugs and get high.

I even committed myself into psychiatric hospitals twice to kick. I was very cooperative. I took the methadone they gave me. I stayed as long as they wanted me to stay, by taking leaves of absence from work.

The director of medicine at the hospital where I worked finally found out that I was using drugs, because one of the psychiatrists in the second mental institution to which I had committed myself had called her and told her. She was very nice about it. She merely said, "Well, you just stay in the hospital and kick, and then we'll take you back."

I stayed two weeks in the psychiatric hospital, and I came out, and that same night I got high again. I really wanted to get off drugs, but I didn't have anything else. Drugs had become everything to me, my reward, my punishment, everything. There just wasn't anything else, and as much as I wanted to be straight, I couldn't see how I could live without the drugs.

I went back to work. They had taken away my job as head nurse, but they let me be on the I.V. team.

By now my habit was worse than ever, and my salary wasn't enough to support it. I got into shoplifting and prostitution. I would shoplift anything I could get my hands on—jewelry, wigs, anything. I'd sell what I'd steal to a fence I'd met through all the junkies I was now hanging out with.

I got into prostitution through another junkie I knew. He had a couple of girls working for him. He had taken a liking to me, so he would make connections for me. When there was money involved, he'd call me.

Eventually, I started selling drugs in the street. I was now into drugs so heavily that I was getting sloppy in my work at the hospital. They could tell that something was wrong. They finally fired me and took away my nursing license.

So here I was no longer a nurse, the profession that had meant so much to me. That was when I really ended up in the street. I was a junkie. My boyfriend had gotten arrested and he was in jail, and I really had no one to turn to. So I shoplifted and I hustled and I shot dope. I also dealt in drugs myself. That was my life.

I was miserable. I wanted out. Even the drugs, even the high, weren't worth it any more.

A junkie's life is complete boredom. It's just emptiness. You're either getting high, or you're high, or you're looking for money to buy drugs, or you're trying to buy drugs. Everything revolves around drugs. You even have no interest in sex or food. The only kind of desire for food that you have is for sweets. For months I lived on orange pop and chocolate ice cream.

One day, a minister came to my door with his wife and daughter. I didn't have anything else to do, since I was bored out of my skull anyway, so I let them in.

They explained that they were "witnessing"—talking to people by going from door to door, talking to people about Christ. I just listened to them very patiently because I didn't have anything else to do. They explained that they were part of a Protestant denomination, Independent Pentecostal.

I was just putting them on for company. But, at the same time, I saw something in their lives. These people were really happy. There was a joy about them. Their daughter was about my age, about twenty, and she radiated. She just glowed. When her father started talking about Christ, he got so excited, I thought, "Wow, what's happening?"

They kept coming back and coming back.

They began to tell me how Jesus could change my life. I couldn't really believe any of it. And yet I wanted them to be around.

They knew that I was a drug addict, that I was shoplifting and into prostitution to make money, and yet they'd do really nice things for me. They wouldn't give me any money, but they'd go out when they saw

I didn't have any food in the house and buy me groceries. I said, "Wow, what's happening?" I'd never run into anything like this before.

Finally they took me to a church meeting in Pittsburgh, a special church meeting presided over by a woman preacher with a healing ministry. I thought the supposed miracle cures she was said to have effected were just part of a kind of mass hypnosis. However, as long as I was in her church, I thought I might as well listen to what she had to say.

I found myself crying and I felt terrible. I felt dirty, I felt filthy.

Suddenly she called me out of the audience! "Just come up here," she said. "I want to pray for you."

I walked up to the front of the church. She put her hands on me. Now I didn't think I believed in God. But I let her put her hands on me and pray for me. We call it being "put under the power." All of a sudden, while her hands were on my shoulders and she was praying for me, I felt a great warmth come over me and I fell to the floor. When I got up I knew I was different. I thought, "Wow, there must be a God if this could happen to me, because I'm not the kind to make a spectacle of myself."

After this service, the minister and his family invited me to go home with them. But I didn't want to.

Instead, I went out and I got high again.

But this time it wasn't the same. My eyes were open. I saw the life I was leading.

I called them up and said, "Look, you say there's a Jesus, and you say He can change my life. I know something happened to me. I don't understand it, I don't know what it was, but something happened to me. I want to get off drugs. If you can help me, please help me."

So they said, "Okay, come on over."

And I went over to their house, and I knew I was going to get sick. I didn't know if I was going to be able to stand it. I told them, "Look, no matter what happens, just keep me here."

And they said, "All right." They also said, "We believe in God. We believe in Jesus and we believe that He heals, that He can save souls, that He can change lives. We're going to pray for you. We're going to ask Him to touch you. We're going to ask Him that you won't be sick."

I said, "Wow, these people are really crazy." But they prayed for me and I wasn't sick. I wasn't sick— and I should have been.

That night in their home, I asked Jesus to come into my heart, and I experienced the same kind of feeling that they already had, this completeness, this wholeness.

The next day they called Brother Benton, who was the head of Teen Challenge in Rhinebeck.

They let me tell my family. Up until this point my family didn't know I was on drugs. They suspected something because of the way I looked, the way I was acting, those few times I visited them. But they never knew for sure. I called them and told them all about it, and I told them that I was going someplace to get help.

Then the minister and his family took me up to Teen Challenge. I have spent eleven months here and it hasn't been easy. But I stayed because I knew it was the place where God wanted me. Gradually, within a couple of weeks, the desire, the need for drugs was gone. I said, "Wow, here I am, living!"

There were no withdrawal symptoms, even though I had had a really bad habit. And here I was, facing life. I was living my life through the power of Christ, through prayer. It was a real change, going into the program, because it was something completely different. I had never seen life like this before.

We pray in the morning, we pray at night. Prayer is my therapy.

Three days a week we have chapel services for an hour. That includes singing and a message from the Bible. After our morning prayers or chapel services, we have two hours of Bible classes. In addition to studying the word of God, we study practical Christian living and Christian conduct. After lunch there is a work period. This consists mainly of housework or work in the garden or on the grounds of the twenty-acre estate.

After supper, we have different kinds of activities. One night they take us shopping, one night we have devotion, another night Bible study, one night a prayer meeting. And sometimes they take us out roller skating, ice skating, or something like that. Saturday we have a free afternoon. And then Saturday evening church service and Sunday church twice.

There is no smoking. They feel that if you can't kick cigarettes, you're never going to kick drugs. We live the Christian life according to the Bible.

We don't believe in dancing. Most of the girls have had trouble with boy-girl relationships. No dancing, no tobacco, no alcohol, no sex. Christ comes into our lives, we don't need these externals, and we know that they're not good for us.

At first it was very difficult. It was only the grace of God that kept me here for that first month. First of all, I wasn't used to religion, and my life wasn't completely committed to Christ. I knew He was real, I knew He had touched me in a miraculous way. He had taken me off drugs without suffering. That was a miracle in itself. I knew this, but yet that personal commitment wasn't there.

Finally, I began to see his power work in my life.

There is love here in Rhinebeck. It is Christ's love showing through these people. They love us as we are. Christ takes us as we are.

Emotionally I was still a child, and I still had to grow, and growing always hurts. But with Christ, He gives us a new beginning. He gives us the strength to go on. And during these eleven months I have had to face myself, to learn to accept myself as I am, as Christ accepts me. He gives me a chance to grow in His love.

I know I will never go back to drugs. I have found the answer. I was hunting for peace. I never knew what it was, but I found it, the happiness, the joy, the completeness, a purpose in my life. It's all there now.

The Lord has come into my life. He has touched me. He has made me whole. I'm going to face trials, I'm going to face temptations, but I don't have to fall because He's there with me.

When I finish here, I'd like to go back into nursing, perhaps as a missionary nurse somewhere. I'll go wherever He wants me to go.

BILL

Cyclazocine is not a magic pill. You must have therapy to go along with it. Otherwise there won't be sufficient motivation to get off drugs and stay off.

Among the newer, more experimental methods of dealing with drug addiction is cyclazocine. As Bill explains, it is an "antagonist" to heroin.

Like Mario, Bill became hooked while serving in the armed forces in Asia. But Bill's service was in peace-time Korea. "Boredom in Korea," says Bill, "was the chief reason that I, along with so many other American soldiers stationed there, got involved with drugs."

He is tall, slender, easy-going, friendly. He now works at a New York City hospital, helping others in the cyclazocine program.

I was born and raised in New York. I went to high school here, where I studied metal trades. But as soon as I was graduated from high school I was drafted into the Air Force and was sent to Korea. The Korean War has been over a long time, but we have always maintained a large number of United States forces in South Korea as a safeguard against possible attack from North Korea.

It was a lot safer than Vietnam as far as getting killed goes, since there was no war and no fighting there. But I guess it really wasn't much safer than Vietnam as far as getting hooked on drugs goes, because it was in Korea that I first got into drugs.

The Americans used to ride around in jeeps with the South Korean soldiers, and it was South Koreans who first introduced me to drugs.

We started with grass in Korea, and then we went to heroin. First we started snorting it, and then skin popping, and finally mainlining. Heroin, like grass, was very easy to get in Korea. And the heroin you get in Korea is very potent. It is also very cheap. For fifty cents you can get enough heroin to last you easily two or three weeks.

Korea was a very new and different type of experience for me. Before I went into the Air Force I had been living with my parents in Bedford-Stuyvesant together with my two sisters. My father is an automobile mechanic and my mother a nurse. We were a close-knit family. Everybody got along fine.

I had never been away from home before. And here I was suddenly some six thousand miles away from home in Korea, eighteen years old and feeling rather homesick and with nothing much to do, especially in my leisure time. The Army, knowing that we had to have something to fill up our leisure hours with, used to arrange for prostitutes to be brought into the compound for us. We would have to sign them in, and then sign them out and escort them outside of the compound. This was not, to me anyway, a very satisfactory way for filling up leisure time.

I would say that boredom in Korea was the chief reason that I, along with so many other American soldiers stationed there, got involved with drugs— boredom and the fact that drugs were so easy to get and so very cheap.

Of course, drugs were always around in that part of Bedford-Stuyvesant where I lived. But I myself had never taken any drugs in America. It wasn't until I got over to Korea that I got involved with drugs.

When I got back home from Korea and got out of the Army, I had a lot of money, what with my overseas pay and mustering-out pay. I had well over six thousand dollars, and there was no need for me to get a job right away. I began hanging around with nothing much to do except look for and find drugs.

In the sixteen months that I had been over in Korea, drugs had really spread in my neighborhood, and most of the fellows I had been brought up with were now really strung out on heroin. Some of the guys had brought the habit home with them from Vietnam. Others had picked it up right here.

I found out as soon as I started using drugs here that there was really a big hassle to cop drugs in New York compared to the way it had been in Korea. And also the stuff that you got on the streets here wasn't nearly as pure or potent as the stuff I had been getting in Korea. Therefore, I had to use double the amount, and sometimes even triple the amount, that I had used over in Korea. That really began running into money, and it wasn't long before I had used up those six thousand dollars I had come back with.

Once I had used up all my savings, and without having a job, I had to take to stealing to support my habit. Eventually I got busted with an assault charge thrown in and ended up in jail.

In jail I met some older fellows who took a liking to me and taught me their trade, which was pick-pocketing. They showed me how to dip, which is how to use your fingers to get a wallet. How to use a razor to cut out a pocket. How to work as a decoy—in other words, how to distract somebody while your partner is picking his pocket. And how to work with somebody else who distracts the victims while you pick their pockets.

After I got out of jail I was able to support my habit much more easily, because I had been trained in the art of being a pickpocket. I would practice pickpocketing mainly at bus stations and airports, because travelers generally have more money on them than other people. I used to make a lot of money. But it was dangerous work because there was always the possibility of getting caught, and I did get caught a few times. Since there was never any assault involved, the sentences I got were generally light. I'd serve sixty days or ninety days and then I'd be out again.

The worst thing about going to jail for pickpocket-ing was the fact that I couldn't get any drugs in jail and I'd have to kick cold turkey. This was really rough. I would get quite sick. Actually, the first few times I had to kick cold turkey were the hardest. After you've kicked cold turkey a few times you sort of get used to it. Later on, when I was arrested and put into jail, it was easier for me to kick cold turkey.

After the last time I was in jail, I went right back into the streets as always. This time, however, I neglected to report to my parole officer. When I finally did report to him, he told me that he would give me a break and not send me back to the penitentiary for parole violation provided I signed myself into the drug program at Beth Israel Hospital. Naturally, I accepted the offer. I figured a hospital would be better than going back to prison.

At Beth Israel, I met a social worker who told me about a new experimental program they were trying involving a new drug called cyclazocine. It wasn't supposed to be addictive the way methadone is. I decided that I'd try this new drug. The program was called Cyclazocine Plus, the plus referring to psychotherapy which you got in addition to cyclazocine.

The program originally was in Greenmont, New York. You have to get detoxified with methadone before you're put on cyclazocine. So I was detoxified at Beth Israel, then shipped up to Greenmont for the Cyclazocine Plus program.

There were twelve of us at a time in a program. The group-therapy sessions there were conducted by a psychiatrist. The purpose was to try to find out the reason we started using drugs, and how motivated we were to stay on the program and get off drugs. The two group-therapy sessions a day were seven days a week for the full three weeks that we were there.

At first, the group-therapy sessions started out very easy and calm in order for those of us who had never had anything like it to get adjusted to it and see what it was like. As the days went by, the sessions became more intensive, finally ending up as encounter therapy, with all of the emotionally charged free expression that is part of encounter therapy.

At the beginning, I didn't like group therapy, especially the encounter part, because I did not like being confronted. But then I saw that everybody else was subjected to being confronted, so I accepted my being confronted, too. It's a lot easier to talk about other people. But when they start talking about you, and telling you what they think of you, why, that's a different story.

I felt that the cyclazocine and the group therapy worked hand in hand. I don't think I would have been helped by one without the other.

After the three weeks at Greenmont, our group of twelve was discharged and sent home and allowed to pick up our cyclazocine every week. It was then up to us to take it every day on our own. In addition, we had group-therapy sessions twice a week at a place in Brooklyn that was connected to the experimental program going on at Greenmont.

I was so happy with the results that I had no desire to go back on drugs and certainly no desire to go back to my life in crime. I needed money to support myself, however, and in order to get it I went on welfare. After a month, a social worker connected with the cyclazocine program helped get me a job at a messenger service.

Unfortunately, the Greenmont psychiatrist died. But by that time they had started a cyclazocine program at a New York City hospital and those of us who had been on his program were transferred there.

When, through spot checking, my employers found out that I had been a drug addict and had a prison record, I was fired. But fortunately I was immediately offered a job working as an aide in the cyclazocine program here at the hospital. Among the things I do, working with the addicts, is run the group-therapy sessions here. Once in a while a psychiatrist will sit in for an hour or so, but most of the time I run the sessions myself. I like this type of work very much. I've been doing it now for two years, and all of this time I've been off drugs.

All this time I've also been taking cyclazocine. Eventually I hope to get off cyclazocine, too. Since, unlike methadone, it is not an addictive drug, it's supposed to be quite easy to stop taking cyclazocine. Over a period of two weeks, they gradually decrease the amount they give you. In a few months I will have completed my three-year stretch on the program, and I hope to be able to get off cyclazocine and be completely drug-free.

Methadone substitutes one dependency in place of another. But cyclazocine is not a dependency. It's what they call an antagonist.

Cyclazocine does effectively stop the need for taking heroin. In fact, if you take heroin while you're on cyclazocine, you get sick. Right after I got on the cyclazocine program I was curious and, just for the fun of it, I tried taking some heroin. I got very sick from it and never took it again.

I think, however, that a very important thing to remember about cyclazocine is that it is not a magic pill. You must have therapy to go along with it. Otherwise there won't be sufficient motivation to get off drugs and stay off.

DANIEL

I had set very high goals for myself. I was looking for some kind of perfection, some kind of answer. I had no real idea who I was. I thought maybe I'd get some insight through drugs.

Daniel, a young black man, is tall, handsome, broad-shouldered, slim-hipped—a varsity athlete. He was born and raised in St. Paul, Minnesota, where he attended a private school before going to Harvard. His father is a professor of physiology.

The interview takes place at Safari House, a drug rehabilitation center on Chicago's South Side. While completing college at the University of Chicago, Daniel is working as assistant director of Safari House.

"I've been off drugs now more than two years," Daniel says. "But I don't consider myself cured, because I don't think there is such a thing as a cure. You can always go back to drugs." The interviewer's impression, however, is that Daniel will never go back to hard drugs.

Soft drugs are something else. He still smokes marijuana.

I was sixteen years old and visiting Harvard when I first smoked marijuana. It was my first experience with any type of drug because, being on the high-school football team, I didn't drink or smoke.

I knew Harvard was certainly a good college. I was proud to be accepted by them. After my visit to Harvard and my first experience with marijuana, I went back to St. Paul and finished out the school year.

I didn't smoke any marijuana or take any other drugs back at St. Paul, mainly because none seemed to be around. But when I went back to Harvard as a freshman my eyes were open to the fact that there were drugs available there.

In addition to playing football in high school, I had learned to play poker and wanted to continue at Harvard. One night there was a knock on my door and one of the students handed me what was actually an engraved invitation for an evening of poker. Very fancy—really far out. Dress was formal or at least semi-formal. That first night of poker at Harvard, I ended up winning three hundred and eighty dollars.

Later at another game I won seven hundred and eighty dollars. One of the guys I was playing poker with ended up owing me a hundred dollars. He mentioned something about pot. I made a deal with him. He paid me only sixty dollars in cash and the rest in pot. And with that large amount of pot I had gotten, I began smoking it regularly.

I still played football. By the end of my first year I had played well enough to make the varsity football team in addition to the varsity wrestling team.

At that time Harvard was considered the LSD capital of the world because that was where Timothy Leary taught and he had been turning his students on to it. A Harvard student told me that he wanted to try it because he had read an article about it in the

Reader's Digest. At that time, possession of LSD was not illegal. It was very easy to come by at Harvard. They charged ten dollars for it in the form of sugar cubes. We tried it.

Jesse, the guy who had sold me the acid, was a weird guy, very tall, and he wore dark glasses. A very strange cat, but he fascinated me. He had his own apartment and always had a lot of girls around. He associated with a lot of non-Harvard people off the campus who were into hard drugs. We became very good friends.

The reason I mention him is because I think that if it weren't for him I might never have become an addict. Jesse was always two steps ahead of me on drugs. When I was smoking pot and experimenting with LSD, he was already shooting speed.

Football, poker, and pot, and that's about all I did. As a result, at the end of my first year, I ended up on probation because my grades were so low.

After that first year, I went back to Minnesota for my summer vacation. When I returned to Harvard in the fall, I took up again with Jesse. Over the summer he had gotten into heroin. I followed Jesse's advice and tried it, mainlining right away. The funny thing was that I did not get high from it that first time, and so I didn't get into it heavily then. Instead, I began shooting speed. Jesse was now dealing in heroin. He got so far into drugs that he dropped out of Harvard and went home to California.

I began getting deeper and deeper into drugs during my second year, especially the second half, and I began falling so far behind in my grades that I made up some sort of excuse to get myself off the hook. I forged a phony doctor's note. However, one of the instructors decided to check up.

As a result of trying to pull that fast one, I was

requested to resign from Harvard, meaning I was kicked out. I knew that this was very bad. But, according to the way Harvard did things, if I worked during the year I was out, I could apply for readmission and be taken back.

I went to Los Angeles to see Jesse. There I began shooting heroin every day. It was easy for me to get the heroin from Jesse because he was dealing in it. He'd get the stuff from Mexico and then he'd sell it in the Los Angeles area.

When I went back to Boston from Los Angeles, I took a hoard of drugs with me. With my contacts in Boston I had no trouble dealing there. By this time I had developed quite a taste for heroin and was an addict. I was shooting it every day. I was able to turn over four or five thousand dollars by dealing in marijuana and spent it all on heroin for myself. I began degenerating rather fast.

Now I was nineteen years old and hooked. A few days before my parents arrived to see me, I got busted in Boston for trying to pass a forged prescription. The druggist was suspicious and called the police. They came right away and arrested me. Being thrown into jail was very frightening, but I was lucky. They let me out that same night on my own recognizance.

As soon as I got out, I was so desperate for dope that I tried passing a bum check. I got caught for that, too. Now everything was suddenly coming down on me. This time I couldn't get out of jail.

When my parents arrived in Boston, that's where they found me, in jail. Naturally, they were very upset. I was in jail for two weeks before my parents were able to get me out. I got quite sick there being without drugs, but I was young and strong and was able to kick cold turkey. I managed to get out of both charges against me, the forged-prescription charge and the bad-check charge, with the understanding that I would leave Boston immediately with my parents and go back to Minnesota.

When I went back home with my parents, I was sick of the whole mess that drugs had gotten me into. I got a job as a computer operator. I really thought that I was free of drugs.

Then one day, I went upstairs to my room and I pulled out my attaché case, which I called my "little drug kit." And I took out a doctor's pad I had stolen and wrote a prescription for speed.

That started it again. I began writing prescriptions for speed rather regularly. Then I wrote a prescription for Dilaudid, which is a synthetic opiate drug like heroin.

I wasn't happy about getting back on drugs. One morning I woke up with such a feeling of disgust that I took the kit and I burned the whole thing. That's how badly I really wanted to be free of drugs. You see, I thought I could kick it myself by doing things like burning the attaché case. I didn't know how sick I was, how much help I needed.

A few weeks later I got the urge for drugs again and found myself in a doctor's office where I stole his prescription pad. In January, I got busted for forging a prescription. This was a terrible thing for my parents, for them to see me in jail again.

They didn't know what it was to be a dope fiend. They thought I had been free of using drugs, that I had cured myself of it, whereas in reality I hadn't. As a matter of fact, at that time I didn't know myself what it meant to be a dope fiend. Anyway, I went to trial and I ended up with two years' probation.

On probation after the trial I was clean for a while. But again it didn't last long. I met somebody in St.

Paul who was a heroin addict. I met him through the social worker to whom I had been assigned as part of my probation. She suggested that I join a group of ex-alcoholics and ex-addicts who were seeking to help themselves, sort of self-help therapy.

Among this group of people was this one guy who was still a heroin addict and had no intention of getting off. He and I used to meet and talk about the possibility of starting some program to help addicts.

One day I suddenly had the urge to get high. I told him about it. He took me over to his house where he gave me some dope and I shot up, and that's how I began using it again. Now I was working again as a computer operator. The fact that I was living at home prevented me from becoming a full-time, full-fledged heroin addict, because I didn't want to hurt my parents any more than I already had. I felt very guilty about the pain I had already caused them and didn't want to cause them any more pain.

After a while, though, they discovered that I was using drugs. We talked about it. I admitted to them that I was back on heroin and that I needed help. They called Synanon.

Synanon at that time was charging five hundred dollars as an admission fee to their program. My parents figured I needed something like Synanon, a kind of hard, structured approach that would help get me together. I wasn't sure, although I realized that I wasn't able to do it on my own. I had tried several times and I had failed.

Meanwhile, the group of ex-alcoholics and ex-addicts that the social worker had sent me to was still meeting in St. Paul. I was still meeting with them. It seemed to me that if they really wanted to get something underway, they would have to learn from one of the self-help organizations that was firmly established and had proven itself, such as Synanon.

Somebody in St. Paul had heard about a very good self-help program in Chicago, and I was selected to be the delegate to Chicago to learn how that program had been set up. And so this was how I came down from St. Paul to Chicago. It was to learn the techniques of the Chicago group called Gateway House.

I was there about a week. I liked what I saw and confessed to the people at Gateway House that I was still very much of an addict and that I needed help. They pulled some strings and got me admitted to their program. I liked the idea of Gateway House because it seemed to be very similar to what I had heard about Synanon. At the same time, it wasn't as far away from my home as Synanon, which then was in Santa Monica, California.

The quarters of Gateway House impressed me very much when I first saw them. They are in a beautiful mansion, a seventy-thousand dollar mansion. And another thing I liked about Gateway House was that, unlike Synanon, I didn't have to pay to get in. My parents would gladly have paid the five hundred dollars that Synanon wanted, but it still would have been a financial hardship for them.

I learned that Gateway had been started by an ex-Synanon person. It was quite similar to Synanon in being that kind of traditional therapeutic community.

When I first entered, I was told I could use methadone for five days to get off heroin, but I didn't want to. I found that even though I had been a heavy heroin user, kicking cold turkey wasn't the way it was in the movies. There was no climbing of the walls, there was no sweating, there were no convulsions.

The worst thing about it was not being able to

sleep at night for a long time, for at least a month. That was really the worst thing. Other symptoms were sniffling and a running nose. It was like having a bad case of flu or a very bad cold but definitely not as dramatic or difficult as I'd heard withdrawal to be, or the way I had seen it in some movies on drugs.

I think kicking is really psychological more than anything else. I myself have found that you can kick the physical part of heroin addiction in three days. It's the psychological addiction that's the tough thing to kick, and that you can't kick in a matter of days. That may take months and probably even years. To cure the psychological addiction to drugs Gateway House used a number of tools similar to those of Synanon. Chief among them were the punishments.

Punishments consisted of shaved heads and wearing signs, such as "Please help me to be nice" or "I'm immature" or "I'm stupid." These were the tools of Synanon and they were used here in Chicago. Some of these tools were definitely needed to effect behavior changes. If a person does something wrong, he has to have some form of punishment to make him realize it, and the shaved head was an effective reminder that he had done something wrong.

I went through Gateway House myself relatively easily. This was for several reasons. First of all, I was able to stay out of the big jackpots, the big troubles. A couple of times I had to wear signs, a couple of times I got "haircuts." This is not the same as having your head shaved. "Haircuts" are verbal. You are yelled at. But I never broke any of the cardinal rules, like the one against violence, so I never had much trouble.

I actually got a lot out of Gateway House. Once I got into the program I realized that I had been bullshitting myself into thinking that I could just pick up what they were doing and bring it back to St. Paul. I realized that I was sick and needed help myself, and so I stayed on for months and months of treatment there.

As for group therapy, I don't think it really helped me that much, mainly because I myself didn't open myself up to it. I didn't give of myself in the group sessions. You see, I felt very strongly that my own rehabilitation really depended upon me.

Whatever you believe in is going to help you. I believed in myself. That's what helped me. If you believe in groups, groups will help you. What's very important to a lot of people is that they need group pressure, and those people were probably helped the most by groups. If you make a commitment to the group then you have to do it—because, if you don't, the next week you'll get a lot of pressure from the group as to why you didn't live up to your commitment.

One good thing the group did for me was that it enabled me to help other people. People broke down and confessed in the group. I did learn to help other people in the group live up to their commitments.

I feel what helped me the most was being isolated from the temptation of drugs. I didn't use any drugs at Gateway House when I felt like it because there was always somebody there I could talk to.

After a few months at Gateway House I started going to school. I transferred my credits from Harvard to the University of Chicago, and switched my major to psychology.

There are three phases of the Gateway therapy. First phase is living in and working in. It's a twenty-four-hour therapeutic community.

After I was there for a few months, I was graduated to the second phase, where I was working out and living in. I was working out by going to the University of Chicago.

After nine months I was in the third phase, which was working out and living out. I was going to school at the University of Chicago. I was also working at a drug clinic as a counselor, and reporting once in a while as part of my third phase to Gateway House.

That's when I smoked pot. I told them about it at Gateway House. I told them that I and another fellow had smoked pot.

When I confessed to smoking pot, they wanted me and this other fellow to move back into the house. I really didn't see anything wrong in what I had done in going back to smoking pot. And I didn't want to go back to living in. I was enjoying very much living out.

Well, we refused to move back into Gateway House and just walked away from the whole thing. That was the best way for me to make it. As a result of breaking away and becoming what they called a "splitee," meaning somebody who's split from Gateway House, I've grown a great deal.

I recognize and thank Gateway House for giving me the foundation upon which to grow, but I suppose it could have been something else. It had to be some sort of isolating factor that was going to keep me completely away from drugs for a while, and Gateway House did do that. Technically, however, I never graduated from Gateway. Members of Gateway are not allowed even to speak to me.

Some people would benefit a great deal from Gateway's rigidity. Others would not.

Here where I'm working now, Safari House, is better than Gateway because it's based more on individual needs. We have a much looser program, a more human program. We don't kick people out so that they can never come back. We don't forbid people here to talk to them. Here we have different phases and we have also a kind of aftercare program, and we try to fit the therapy to the person's needs.

There's no program in the world that can do anything for anybody who really doesn't want to get off drugs. The all-important thing is that you have to want to get off drugs. That's the first step.

After that, what you need is a change of environment. It doesn't have to be a totally new environment, a twenty-four-hour encompassing environment. It can be an environment that you know is there when you need it, when you want it—something you can commute to. Whenever you get bored or you feel a craving for drugs, you should know that this environment is ready for you, that it's something you can go to whenever you want.

As for starting in with drugs in the first place, I don't know what made me do it. I guess I was looking for something.

I don't think my parents were to blame. I think that my parents were actually very good parents.

I myself had set very high goals for myself. I was always dissatisfied with what I did in one way or another. I was looking for some kind of perfection, some kind of answer. I thought maybe I'd get some insight through drugs.

I had no real idea who I was. I really didn't have any identity as a black person, and yet I didn't have any identity as a non-black person.

I didn't know what I wanted to get out of school. I didn't want to be a doctor or a lawyer or anything.

Boredom was also a factor. I was certainly bored studying. That's why I was looking for excitement. I found it in poker and drugs. You see, all of the square alternatives bored me. At Harvard, dating on a Friday night, going to all your classes, chatting with the guys in the lunchroom—all of that turned me off.

When I started at Harvard, not that many people were into drugs. Suddenly, because I was using drugs, I was part of a very exclusive group.

I've been off drugs now more than two years, but I don't consider myself cured, because I don't think there is such a thing as a cure. You can always go back to drugs. You've always got to be aware of the danger of going back to drugs and what circumstances can lead you back to drugs. Some of the circumstances which can lead you back are getting hooked up with friends who are drug users, living with an old lady who is a drug user, letting boredom catch up with you.

One way of coping with boredom is by keeping busy. I go to school full time now. I have a B average at the University of Chicago. In addition, I work eight hours a day here at Safari House on this drug program. So I am pretty busy.

I find my work here at Safari House more interesting than school. I am now the assistant director of Safari House. However, I don't plan to make working in drug rehabilitation my life's work.

I'm basically still the same person. But before, because I didn't know who I was or what I wanted, I went into drugs. Now I still don't know who I am or where I'm going or what I want. But this time I'm not letting it stump me. What I am doing is trying to keep all the alternatives open.

SUSAN

I realized that I never got anything out of taking the tranquilizers, the amphetamines, the barbiturates. I got off drugs because I was able to suddenly grow up a bit and face reality. I also got tired of serving time in prison.

Susan is from Beverly Hills, California. Her father, who inherited his wealth, never had to work for a living.

Susan's interview takes place at the Vinewood Residence for Girls in Hollywood, a "halfway house" for drug addicts who have been in jail and are now on state parole.

Susan is wearing sneakers, blue jeans and a peasant blouse. Her dark hair is long and loose, her voice is low, and her manner is easy.

I got into the drug scene alone. I never ran with any-body who was a user.

I'm an only child. I come from a wealthy family. My father had been left a lot of money from my grandfather, who was a very wealthy corporation lawyer, and never had to do anything for a living. For a short while my father was a gentleman farmer, but most of the time all he did was sit around on his ass.

I had a pretty screwed-up childhood, despite the big house where we lived in Beverly Hills. But money was never a problem. They gave me whatever I wanted.

My mother is about as screwed up as they come, but somehow her neuroses don't send her to jail. My dad is very passive, my mother super-aggressive. I was closer to my dad than I was to my mom. I could get along with him much better.

I can't say that it was all my parents' fault. I feel that the way they raised me may have contributed to my using drugs. But it was really I who made the decisions. *I* took the drugs. They didn't *make* me.

My folks were hung up on all of the upper-class values. The kid had to go to college and that whole scene, so I went.

I first started using drugs at college. I was carrying a very heavy schedule and started using ampheta-mines to keep up with the heavy amount of studying I had. I was a history major and hoped to work in the Foreign Service department of the government after I got out. After using amphetamines for a while, I started taking downers, or barbiturates, to go to sleep.

It was very easy to get pills at college in Missouri, just as it's easy to get pills anywhere. Mostly I got amphetamines and barbiturates by hustling doctors.

It was easy. I never bought anything on the black market. You go in to the doctors and you give them a line of bull about how you're nervous and can't sleep, or you are depressed, and they'll give you whatever you want.

In my third year of college I was down at the University of Arizona for a semester. I was majoring in Asian history, with Chinese history as my specialty, and they had a good course on the subject. I really thought I had all of my shit together. I had prescriptions in Tucson and Palm Springs. I thought I'd make that circle run every couple of weeks. I had my own car. It would be easy to get around.

The thing that really hit me was that I was getting strung out on tranquilizers at the time—Equanil in particular. A lot of people think because it's a tranquilizer there's nothing to it. Bullshit, you can get strung out on it. I was.

Somehow, one night, in the middle of watching television and thinking how bizarre what I was watching was, I suddenly realized how bizarre my own life was. I still hadn't realized that I was an addict. To me addiction was heroin addiction. I honestly didn't know that people could get strung out on tranquilizers. I decided, "Hey, this isn't the way I want to live my life."

I took all the pills I had and I threw them out.

A few hours later I went into convulsions. I mean, I started kicking and I kicked and kicked and kicked for days. At first what was happening didn't hit me. I knew I was sick. I thought I had the flu or some damn thing like that. Finally, with these severe convulsions I was having, I realized that this was addiction.

I began reading books on drugs, and I learned that you can get addicted to things other than heroin.

However, I didn't stay off drugs very long, perhaps only two or three weeks. I got right back on them again, but at the same time I entered therapy with a psychiatrist. This doctor suggested I finish the semester at school.

I decided to try to finish the semester, but I was unable to. I was so strung out that I had to drop out and lose credit.

I came home and stopped using pills again and flipped out. I started hallucinating.

Then I was off drugs for four or five months. I began drinking heavily. I kept up the routine of pills or booze or both for a couple of years until I got busted on a burglary charge.

I was so desperate for drugs that I took a crowbar from our garage. Wearing only my nightgown, I went down to this drugstore and smashed into the place with the crowbar. This set off alarms, and the cops came right away and busted me. There I was only in my nightgown, this little dingy duck that I was, weighing ninety-three pounds. But the cops acted as though it was a real big bust. They threw me up against the counter. There were about six cops, and they all had their guns pulled. I didn't know what was happening.

One of them told me, "You know, you could have gotten yourself killed."

I thought to myself, "What the hell is he talking about, man?"

I mean, I didn't have weapons or anything.

The cops took me to jail. I was only there for twelve hours when my parents bailed me out.

When we got home my parents were all over the walls. They were screaming at me, "Look what you've done to us!"

I tried to tell them, "Hey, I'm really scared. I don't

know what's happening. I feel like my whole life's being blown up. I really need help."

But they didn't want to hear it. They didn't want to hear anything except their own screaming about what I had done to them.

At the time I was living with my folks and taking a couple of classes at U.C.L.A., but I wasn't really seriously into my studies. I was completely freaked out. My parents knew about it, but they didn't want to know about it. Their attitude was, "If we don't look at it or talk about it, it will go away." They hassled the hell out of me. They kept telling me what a rotten dirty bitch I was, how I was ruining their lives—just a whole lot of bullshit.

At the same time I must admit they did try to get me some help. They sent me to another psychiatrist.

I was in unbelievably bad shape. I was freaking out constantly, having hallucinations without knowing when they'd appear. Sometimes they'd appear even when I wasn't taking drugs. I thought this psychiatrist my parents had sent me to was very good. He brought me a long way, but not far enough. Just when we got to the part of my becoming aware of my feelings, I suddenly got scared. The result was that I started to get into drugs more heavily than ever before. Then I began freaking out all over the place.

I got a probation violation on that burglary charge because I never reported. All I was interested in doing was taking drugs, running and using. At this time I got heavily into speed and heavily into downers. I got money for my drugs by forging checks.

In November of 1968 they caught up with me and I was sent to the California Rehabilitation Center. It's a state program for narcotics addicts rather than just a straight prison. I was in the center for twenty-one months and all that time I was off drugs. I didn't have any withdrawal symptoms like convulsions because I kicked before I was committed. Actually it isn't that tough to kick, to get clean. What's really tough is to stay clean.

After I got out, I went back to drugs again. What followed was a series of hospitalizations because I went back into therapy and my doctor would see that I was loaded all the time. And so he suggested that I go into a hospital. The hospitalizations didn't do any good. After I got out, I'd go right back to drugs.

I got a job, night manager of a motel, and one night I robbed the cash register to get money for drugs. After I robbed the motel, I started running. But then, after two weeks, I decided to turn myself in. I didn't like what was happening. I realized that I didn't really want to do it, but just hadn't been able to help myself.

I got sent to the state prison for ninety days. And then from state prison I got transferred back to the California Rehabilitation Center. Actually, I preferred being in the state prison because most of the narcotic addicts in the CRC program were hikes, or heroin addicts.

That's when I seriously started thinking about really never using any kind of drugs again. I realized that I never got anything out of taking drugs, out of all the drugs I had taken, the tranquilizers, the amphetamines, the speed, the barbiturates. I had taken them because of the great need I had to be accepted. And dope fiends very easily accept anyone who's on drugs, no matter what drugs they're on, whether it's heroin or speed or anything.

Another reason I took drugs might be my attitude toward sex. I was always very afraid of sex. In fact, I still am. The only times I could have any sexual relations was after I had taken a lot of drugs that would loosen my inhibitions. Then I'd go out and have sex with some guy, and under the influence of drugs I'd think it was being very cool. But actually I wasn't enjoying it at all.

I still have this problem with sex, which is one of the reasons I am going to go into a new kind of therapy. At least now I can accept the fact that I'm hung up on sex without having to run to drugs to deal with my hang-up. Instead, I hope to be able to deal with it through this new kind of therapy.

I don't like to generalize, but I'll say this. You'll find that anybody who is into drugs has some kind of hang-up with sex. Whether they'll cop to it or not, it's true. People who use drugs don't have a normal sex life. Either they're overdoing it with sex or they're not doing it at all.

I would say that in my case I got off drugs through no therapy, or at least through no formal therapy at all. I got off drugs because I was able to suddenly grow up a bit and face reality.

Of course I also got tired of serving time in prison. I had been twenty-one months in the California Rehabilitation Center for my first offense of breaking into that drugstore. And I had served three months in the state prison last year, and then some months again in the center. This kind of halfway house where I am now is for my second offense, the grand-theft charge when I robbed the cash register at the motel.

It's true that I was getting tired of serving time, but that really wasn't why I quit drugs. I don't have too many regrets about the time I've served in prison because it was part of my life that just had to be lived. Now I'm feeling that things are just beginning, that things are really opening up for me. I am clean. I'm feeling all together.

I feel great about my job. I am working right now as a legal secretary for an attorney. It's a hard job and a lot of work. It's a big hassle and I'm working a nine-to-five job, which I said I would never do. But here I am doing it and actually enjoying it—the hard work, the regular hours, everything. I'm supporting myself. I'm responsible for myself.

Eventually I want to go back to college and get my B.A. I don't have many courses to take to do that.

I consider *myself* the therapy that got me off drugs. However, I must also give credit to the various forms of group therapy that I had both in the state prison and the California Rehabilitation Center and even here at this halfway house that I live in now. These various groups did give me some insight. I was an only child and never had the by-play between children that comes from sibling rivalry. I did get some of that in the various groups I attended. There's no question but that they helped.

I was in all sorts of groups including encounter groups where there was the typical yelling and screaming. I must say that I prefer groups where people sit around and talk rather than scream at one another, because I'm the type of person who clams up when there's any evidence of hostility.

I seemed to get more out of groups when I was trying to help somebody else than when others were trying to help me. When I was trying to help somebody else, I could identify with him and see that his problems were a lot like my own problems, and this would give me some insights.

Even the individual psychiatry I'd had from time to time helped. But there is no therapy that's going to help, no therapy in the world could possibly help, unless the addict is ready to be helped and really wants to be helped. Parents of addicts are always looking for the one answer, the magic solution to drug addiction. There is no one answer and certainly no magic solution.

Synanon out here in L.A. has helped some people, but it hasn't helped everyone. Synanon can't help, nothing can help, if the addict himself isn't ready to be helped, if he isn't ready to listen.

That's the discouraging thing about drug addiction. Mimi, who runs the Vinewood Residence for Girls, this halfway house here in L.A., has been working with addicts for ten, fifteen years. She has seen them go in and out of different therapies and they're still hooked after ten or fifteen years, because they really weren't ready to listen and be helped and to take the responsibility for their own lives. Once you really are ready to be helped, then you can be.

I myself am going into another type of therapy next week. It's called primal therapy, and it's been developed by a California psychiatrist. I don't know much about it. Mimi knows about it and she's the one who recommended it for me.

I'm going into it for other reasons, not for drug addiction, because I feel now that I'm off drugs for good.

Author's Note

The drug-treatment centers mentioned in this book, all under their real names, are typical of hundreds of treatment centers throughout the United States. The National Clearinghouse for Drug Abuse Information (operated by the National Institute of Mental Health) furnishes information about facilities available for counseling or treatment in or near specific communities.

The address of the National Clearinghouse for Drug Abuse Information is 5600 Fishers Lane, Rockville, Maryland 20852.

Acknowledgments

Dr. Harry R. Potter, one of the first to encourage me to do this book, gave me invaluable assistance by introducing me to the excellent drug program at Roosevelt Hospital in New York, where Dr. Emil Pascarelli, director of community medicine, and Irwin Levine, director of the adolescent drug program, were most helpful.

Commissioner Meyer H. Diskind, Dale Wright, Tom Stevens and Pat Paterson of the New York State Narcotic Addiction Control Commission were cooperative in letting me investigate the New York state program and interview freely at the commission's Mt. Morris facility in Harlem. Ronald Tamburri, facility coordinator at New York's Horizon Center, funded by city and federal grants, was similarly helpful.

Another cooperative city program was that of Los Angeles' Vinewood Residence for Girls. At nearby Santa Monica, Synanon opened its doors to me and let me roam at will with my tape recorder.

El Vicio in Santa Fe, New Mexico; Cenikor in Lakeland, Colorado; Safari House in Chicago, Illinois; Project Renaissance in Westport, Connecticut; Teen Challenge in Rhinebeck, New York; the Youth Center in Washington, D.C.;

the U.S. Veterans Administration in New York; Daytop Village in New York—all were open, friendly and cooperative.

Not every treatment center I approached was equally friendly. One refused to have anything to do with me. The director of another said he would cooperate only in return for a financial contribution. A staff member at a third center stopped me in the middle of an interview and threw me out. At a fourth, an ex-addict discouraged me from continuing there by firing a revolver in my general direction.

My thanks go also to Dr. Jerome Jaffe, Frank Quintana, Dr. Daniel Rednor, Dr. Richard B. Resnick, Charles Devlin, Dr. Robert L. Dupont, Jim Fair, and the many others who welcomed me to the treatment centers I visited throughout the country.

Special thanks to my editors, Wilma Ross and Janet Finnie, and to Dr. John Rush, Deputy Director of the White House Special Action Office for Drug Abuse Prevention, for their enthusiasm, encouragement and assistance.

Above all, I am deeply indebted to the thirteen young men and women who were hooked and who let me use their stories for this book. With all my heart I hope they make it.

HAROLD FLENDER

About Harold Flender

HAROLD FLENDER is a novelist and film maker. His first novel, Paris Blues, *became a successful motion picture starring Paul Newman and Sidney Poitier. He is also the author of* Rescue in Denmark, *the true story of the rescue of the Danish Jews during World War II, which he turned into a prizewinning documentary film for CBS-TV. His film dramatization of Stephen Vincent Benét's* John Brown's Body *won the B'nai B'rith Human Rights Award.*

He has taught film writing at Columbia University and the New School in New York; at the University of Dakar in Senegal; and at the Centre d'Etudes de Radiodiffusion-Télévision Française in Paris.

Born and raised in New York, he has worked in forty-nine states, in Europe, Africa, and the Midwest, and was a Fulbright scholar for a year in Paris. He lives in Manhattan with his wife and two children.